POLITICAL THOUGHT

VENKATA MOHAN

ISBN 979-888503533-0

Contents

Contents

Contents

Preface

Seeking to create an ideal city-state that would have virtuous as well as happy people, Plato set out a noble task for Western political thought. Did we succeed in fulfilling that task? On reflection, we seem to have got distracted and may have lost the plot. We did make progress but only a fraction of what our scientific progress would have enabled had we been concerned of the human soul as much as we had been of material wealth.

We created economic systems that run on greed and political systems that seem to pit one man's lust for power with another's. And finally, mankind stands confused with conflicting goals: economic growth threatening the very survival of man. This book is an invitation for reflection on our collective journey, as revealed through the thought of various thinkers from Plato to Habermas.

Hope you enjoy reading.

Venkata Mohan

November 2021

Plato

Plato

CHAPTER ONE

From Just Soul to Just City

Plato (427–347 BCE) is one of the foundational figures in Western political thought. He was a disciple of Socrates and learnt many important concepts from him. Plato was born during the time of the Peloponnesian War (431–404) and lived through this war that the Greek historian Thucydides described. Plato belonged to Athens and after Athens was defeated in this war, an oligarchy ruled the city-state during 404 and 403. This oligarchy included some members of Plato's family. It was then deposed and replaced by a democratic regime that later executed Socrates. Plato founded the Western world's first university, called the Academy, in 387 BCE. It lasted for a thousand years. His main political work is The Republic, written from 380 to 370 BCE, and contains all the important ideas of his political thought.

What is Plato's central idea? Socrates equated goodness with happiness. And if one is happy being good, one's interests match with those of the society. The unity of goodness and happiness is something that is only understood when one has the knowledge which comes through reasoning. A huge part of this knowledge is the knowledge of self. Socrates' focus was on the individual, and Plato extended Socrates' ideas to a political system.

Justice is an important concept to Socrates, it is a combination of goodness and happiness. Plato wanted to find out what is a just political system, and specifically a just city because Ancient Greece had many city-states. It became a kingdom only much later.

The Socratic method is a method of enquiry consisting of questioning, reasoning, and counter-questioning to arrive at the truth. The Republic consists of dialogues in which Socrates discusses philosophical matters with many other people. He doesn't give speeches. If one person defines something in a particular way, Socrates questions it and this starts a chain of reasoning. The Socratic method is called dialectics, which means the resolution of contradictions.

In his Republic, Plato created many characters that question Socrates, making various assertions, and Socrates responds to them. However, we don't know what the real Socrates said and what Plato wanted to say through Socrates. The Socrates portrayed in Plato's Republic is, one can say, largely Plato's Socrates. By convention, scholars take him as Plato rather than as the actual Socrates. It is Plato's understanding of Socrates as well as his extension of Socratic thought that we get to see in The Republic.

The idea of justice

The Republic starts with the discussion on justice, various definitions are offered, and Socrates rejects them all. Socrates explains what justice is, within a person or soul. Justice is harmony, a proper relationship between parts, out of which goodness and happiness come.

Plato says what should lead a soul is wisdom, which is superior to courage and honor and also superior to desires like desires for sex, food, comfort and money. For example, if we simply eat going by our desire without any control then our eating becomes a problem, we may end up overeating which leads to disease. Justice within a soul refers to the right relationship between the parts. In a just soul, there is harmony, a proper relationship in terms of the hierarchy of its elements. Wisdom should be higher than bodily pleasures.

The topmost aspect of the soul is the reasoning part, which is the source of wisdom and truth. Next comes the spirited part, which is the source of honour and courage. Then there is the appetitive part, which refers to our desire for money, sex and other bodily pleasures. Temperance means the right relationship between these parts.

The reasoning part, the spirited part, and the appetites are there in every person. But in some people, the reason may be dominant, in some the spirited part, and in some others the appetites. Plato says that a just city is created if there is a hierarchical relationship across these three classes of people living in that city.

Reasoning-oriented people should be the rulers, spirit-oriented people should be the warriors, and the remaining people like traders and farmers are assumed to be appetites-oriented, constituting the lowest rung. The hierarchy of qualities in a just soul is extended to the hierarchy of classes in a just city.

Some people may have the element of reason in dominance, but could there be a whole group of people like that who can be selected? Plato thinks so. If one component is dominant in a person, the other components would not be important because of which people can be classified into three classes. "We know that anyone whose predilection tends strongly in a single direction has correspondingly less desire for other things, like a stream whose flow has been diverted into another channel."

The first class is philosophers, who should be the rulers. The second class is auxiliaries or the warriors. The third class is the productive class, constituting farmers, craftsmen, and traders. The first two classes combined are also called the guardians.

All the classes put together have wisdom coming from the philosopher-kings, courage coming from the auxiliaries, and there should be temperance in the society. Temperance is not the one coming from the third class alone, it is about the acceptance of every class of their place in the society. "Justice is doing one's own task and not meddle with that of others."

"When the whole soul accepts the leadership of the philosophical part, and there is no internal conflict, then each part can do its job and be just in everything it does, and in particular can enjoy its own pleasures and thus reap as much benefit and truth from pleasure as is possible for it."

"When one of the other two parts is in control, however, it not only fails to attain its own pleasure, but it also forces the other parts to go after unsuitable, false pleasures."

Giving too much importance to the appetites, Plato thinks, can bring disasters. The soul in which this appetite element is dominant is called the tyrannical soul. "Nothing is too outrageous: a person acts as if he were totally lacking in moral principle and unhampered by intelligence. In his dreams, he does not stop at trying to have sex with his mother and with anyone or anything else – man, beast, or god. He is ready to slaughter anything; there is nothing he wouldn't eat."

Plato's description of what a just soul is may be right. But he extends it to a city. His just city is the one with the right relationship between the three classes. Is such an extension valid?

Think on it

1. What is the political context that shaped Plato's thought?
2. What is the main teaching of Socrates?
3. What is the central concern of Plato in The Republic?
4. What is meant by the unity between ethics and politics?
5. What is meant by dialectics?
6. What are the three parts of the soul?
7. How is the concept of a just soul extended to a just city?
8. What are the three classes in a just city?
9. What should be the relationship among the classes in a just city?

CHAPTER TWO

Will the Republic Be Ruled by Wisdom or a Wise Man's Son?

Plato discusses the creation of just city-states in The Republic. He considers a just city-state to be one with a hierarchical arrangement of three classes of people, the philosopher-kings, the auxiliary class (warriors) and the producer class. People are selected into the classes based on their innate nature. There is some similarity here with the Indian caste system. In the caste system too, various castes are hierarchically arranged, each caste must do its duty and understand its place in the total system.

But people are born into their caste, whereas Plato's classes are more flexible. Still, the problem with Plato's arrangement is that when the individuals are selected into a class based on their nature, there is nothing to prevent an individual from changing. At the time of recruitment, one may be good at reasoning, but does it mean he will continue to excel in reasoning all through his life? He may give in to his baser appetites at some point.

Moreover, are people so different from each other that some are reasoning-oriented, some spirit-oriented and some appetite-oriented? Can people be classified so distinctly?

And what happens to the children of these people? Plato assumes that the children of the reason-oriented people will also be reason-oriented and so on. The children of one class will remain a part of their class, but Plato says if a person doesn't show the attributes of his class, he can be shifted to a more suitable class. So if a reasoning child is found in the producer class, he can be shifted, but such cases are treated more as exceptions rather than regular.

Role of education

Plato knows that the tendencies one is born with are only some of the many variables that shape oneself. He believes in the role of education. The purpose of this education is to promote justice and goodness. Here the priority should be given to the guardian class, and especially to the children of the philosopher-kings.

The philosopher-kings must reset the society. "The immediate difference between them and others is that they would refuse to touch a city or an individual, or to write laws unless they either take over a clean board or clean it themselves."

"All in the city over ten years of age they will send into the country. Then they will take the children in hand, away from their parents' way of life, and bring them up in their own ways and by their own laws. This is the quickest and the easiest way to establish the city and constitution we have discussed, for it to be happy and to confer the greatest benefits upon the people among whom it may be established."

Early education is very important. "The most important stage of any enterprise is the beginning, especially when something young and sensitive is involved. You see, that is when most of its formation takes place, and it absorbs every impression that anyone wants to stamp upon it."

In Ancient Greece, Homer's Iliad and Odyssey were looked upon as the Bible would be in the later Christian societies. Plato objected to Homer's books because he did not agree with their morals. Plato believed that the characters in myths and epics play an important role in developing virtue in children at a very early stage. "He would find offensive the things he ought to find offensive. Fine things would be appreciated and enjoyed by him. And then reason would be greeted like an old friend when it did arrive because anyone with this upbringing would be more closely affiliated with rationality than anyone else."

Educated parents produce better children, and society keeps on improving itself over generations. "A good education system, if maintained, engenders people of good character; and then people of good character, if they are in their turn receive the benefits of an education of this kind, become even better than their predecessors in every respect, but especially – as is the case with other creatures too – in that they produce better children."

The would-be philosopher-kings must be carefully selected and tested at different stages. At around age 20, they get to learn mathematics and sciences – arithmetic, geometry, solid geometry, astronomy and harmonics. Finally, at age 50, after about 15 years of administrative experience, they are expected to get a glimpse of the Forms of the Good, which means seeing goodness in its abstract form and not just in concrete instances.

Communism

In any society, the rulers are generally associated with wealth. Plato did not want his philosopher-kings to accumulate power and wealth. The rulers are identified based on their reasoning orientation. Their joy lies in reasoning and exercising thought, and not in dominating people. They will rule not for the sake of power but as a duty. And to ensure that those desiring wealth do not come to rule, Plato says that the class of philosopher-kings should be deprived of property and even of the family so that only those people who are mainly interested in philosophy will be the rulers.

Both the guardian classes will have common messes and live together like soldiers in a camp, with minimum facilities. They are not to own gold and silver, they own only their weapons, and there is no privacy in their lives. They live on rations, fixed amounts of essential goods will be given to them.

The people of the third class will live normal lives, possessing property and land. Plato's communism, therefore, does not imply any kind of 'ownership of means of production ', it applies only to the top two classes and means making them live in an austere commune.

Though the guardian classes will be deprived of family, there will be temporary marriages, done mainly for the sake of reproduction. These marriages would happen in such a way that the best get to breed the best. There is no room for love affairs and such. The state will arrange the mating process in what would seem like a lottery fashion, but the matching is rigged in a way that the best would breed the best. The children would not know their parents.

There would be no sex outside marriage among the people of the guardian classes during the reproductive years. But this is not out of any moral considerations, as they are allowed to freely indulge in sex after they reach a certain age.

The abolition of private families in the guardian classes will "prevent them from tearing the city apart by using the expression 'mine' to refer not to the same thing, but to various things." 'My house' of one is different from the 'my house' of another. Therefore the notion of 'mine' has to be eradicated. "All regard the same things as within their circle of interest, tend in the same direction, and feel pleasure and pain as much as possible under the same circumstances."

In this arrangement, women are not discriminated against. They have the same opportunities as the men, to be educated as well as to rule. Women may be inferior to men in certain ways but not as philosopher-kings. This means there would be philosopher-queens.

Why would some people agree to live in such deprived conditions, bereft of property and family? Because they would get their incentives in the form of their achievements and honour. "The guardians' victory is more splendid, and their upkeep by the general populace is more thorough-going. The fruit of their victory is the preservation of the whole community, their prize the maintenance of themselves and their children with food and all of life's essentials. During their lifetimes they are honoured by their community, and when they die they are buried in high style."

Also, once the philosopher-kings or philosopher-queens reach a mature age and understand the Forms, they "do not want to engage in human business: there is nowhere else their minds would ever rather be than in the upper region." They would rule only because they are capable of ruling, and do not take any particular pleasure in it. They rule "not as something splendid, but as a duty."

Evaluation

A soul should be led by wisdom. We can understand that. But can there be an exclusive class of wise people, who can be clearly chosen? Can there be such an education which would really impart lasting wisdom to young people? And could this wisdom be inherited? Would the children of these wise people and the children's children be predominantly wise too? Plato's extension of the Socratic concept of a just soul to a just city seems to be flawed, as his ideal state will in time be ruled not by wise people but only by the children of these wise people who may or may not be wise.

Think on it

1. What is the difference between Plato's classes and India's castes?
2. Why role does education play in Plato's ideal state?
3. How is communism in Plato's state different from communism as we know it in the 20thcentury?
4. How does Plato's communism promote goodness in society?
5. Would Plato's ideal state really produce goodness and happiness in society?

CHAPTER THREE

Plato's Theory of Forms

Let us discuss Plato's ideas on what constitutes reality and the political implications of these ideas. Plato believes that our world is unreal. He explains this unreality by an analogy of some prisoners in a cave who can see only the shadows that the outside objects cast on the cave walls. They can never see the objects themselves. Before looking further into Plato's analogy, let us consider a more familiar example of faulty perception in the story of the elephant and the blind men.

Each blind man touches only a part of the elephant and thinks it is something else. One man touches the tail and says it's a rope, another touches the ear and says it is a fan, somebody touches a leg and says it is a pillar, somebody touches the main body and says it is a wall. Any normal person can look at the whole elephant and see how the blind men are mistaken.

How can he explain the elephant to the blind men? One cannot communicate the experience of vision as such to a blind person. If someone says, 'This is beautiful', the blind man may wonder if he means it is tasty. Similarly, some people have seen the truth, how does a person who knows the truth convey it to the people who do not know it and can not know it?

There are some political implications here. The majority of people have wrong notions about the world around them, but the one who knows the truth is a rare person and would be in the minority. And the minority may not get a voice in a political system like democracy.

Allegory of the cave

Plato's allegory of the cave is a little more complicated than the story of the blind men and the elephant. There are prisoners in a cave, tied to the wall, who cannot even turn their heads sideways. They cannot escape. Only a little light seeps into the cave, and these people can only see the moving shadows on the wall.

And because these prisoners have been so all along, they don't even have an idea of the real objects or a world outside the cave. They think those shadows are the real objects in themselves. And to pass the time, they have created some games around these shadows, like a contest about who would be able to predict the appearance of certain shapes or their movement. Those who seem to know more about the shadows get more respect.

But if one of these prisoners manages to escape, and gets to see the real world outside the cave, along with the sun and the entire landscape, he would become a realized person. He would be shocked by his ignorance when he was in the cave. He may now want to go back to the cave and help his friends.

Suppose he goes back and tells them about the world outside, would they even believe him? They might treat him as if something wrong happened to him when he went away from them. If he tries to make them free and take them outside too, they might not let him. Plato says, "Would not they grab hold of anyone who tried to set them free and kill him?" A clear reference to Socrates.

In terms of the politics in a democracy, this is a situation of many vs one – the one who knows the truth versus the many who take the shadows to be the real things. How can a political system run on the truth when the opinions of the people and the truth differ from each other so much?

Theory of Forms

What is Plato suggesting through this allegory of the cave? What is this thing called reality? This is what Plato's theory of Forms is about. It says there are real objects and their shadows, and the shape of the shadows depends on many things. The shadows are changing in flux, whereas the reality is unchanging.

The changing objects in our world that are accessible to our senses are but reflections of certain unchanging entities in an abstract world, the world of Ideas. These entities are called Forms. A table is a sensible object, but a rectangle is a Form. A table may look like a perfect rectangle, but if you measure it minutely there will be flaws because there can be perfection only in the Form. Plato says the table is a "participant" in the Form of the rectangle. Forms are ideals and abstractions, while the objects of the sensible world appear real to us.

The things in the sensory world are changing and flawed, but the Form is something perfect. And Plato thinks there are Forms for everything. Even things that are abstract in our world have corresponding Forms. There are many good things in our world, and there is a Form for goodness. The philosophers are expected to know these Forms. A philosopher-king is expected to have seen the Form of goodness particularly.

To Plato, his theory of Forms is true of physical objects as well as abstract concepts such as goodness. Plato says that the Form of the Good should be recognized as "responsible for everything right and fine, whatever the circumstances, and that in the visible realm it is the progenitor of light and the source of light, and in the intelligible realm it is the source and provider of truth and knowledge." Just like the Sun is the source of all light in this world, the Form of Goodness is the source of all the truth and wisdom in our world.

Aristotle's criticism

Many people have wondered about the true nature of these Forms, if at all they really exist. In his Metaphysics, Aristotle explains how this theory originated, "The theory of Forms occurred to those who enunciated it because they were convinced as to the true nature of reality by the doctrine of Heraclitus, that all sensible things are always in a state of flux; so that if there is to be any knowledge or thought about anything, there must be certain other entities, besides sensible ones, which persist. For there can be no knowledge of that which is in flux."

Aristotle asks, how can we be sure that there is something like a Form or an Idea as it is also called? Even if such things exist, should we have to know about them? What could be the exact use of knowing the Form of the Good? Aristotle dismisses the theory of Forms as stated by Plato.

Aristotle says in his Nicomachean Ethics, "It is hard, too, to see how a weaver or a carpenter will be benefited in regard to his own craft by knowing this 'good itself' or how the man who has viewed the Idea itself will be a better doctor or general thereby. For a doctor seems not even to study health in this way, but the health of man, or perhaps rather the health of a particular man; it is individuals that he is healing."

A carpenter makes a chair, why should he know the Form of a chair in order to be a better carpenter? And how would he do it? A doctor tries to get a person healed, should he know about the Form of health? What is the point of treating real-world objects such as chairs as mere shadows that participate in their Form?

How to be good is more important than obtaining any knowledge of the Form of goodness. Aristotle says, "We are inquiring not in order to know what virtue is, but in order to become good since otherwise our inquiry would have been of no use."

A carpenter need not know anything about the Form of a right angle, someone studying geometry may be more concerned with it. "For a carpenter and a geometer investigate the right angle in different ways; the former does so in so far as the right angle is useful for his work, while the latter inquires what it is or what sort of thing it is; for he is a spectator of truth."

And subjects like ethics and politics are inexact, we don't need to know anything like definite Forms in their context. We can do with approximations to the truth. "We must be content, then, in speaking of such subjects and with such premises to indicate the truth roughly and in outline, and speaking about things which are only for the most part true, and with premises of the same kind, to reach conclusions that are no better." In general, Plato spoke for abstract knowledge, and Aristotle favoured empirical knowledge.

Seeds of totalitarianism

What is the connection between Plato's theory of Forms and his ideal city? As we have seen, the philosopher-kings are expected to know the Form of goodness. That is why only they have the right to rule. Others know only the shadows of goodness. The man who escapes the cave and sees the sun knows the reality, and a philosopher-king is such a person. The philosopher-kings have the right to make policies, rule and even manipulate the people if there is any need. But such an attitude about the power some people can rightfully wield can give rise to totalitarianism.

In his book The Open Society and Its Enemies, Karl Popper denounces Plato's Republic. The Republic suggests that there are absolute moral truths by which people should live. This does not bode well for an open society. Because only the philosopher-kings are supposed to know the truth, they can subordinate an individual to the state in any way they think is right. For example, in the process of mate selection, the lots would be drawn in a rigged manner as seen fit by the philosopher-kings.

According to Plato, the philosophers or the rulers have the right to create myths too in order to make people believe in certain things. For example, a myth would be created that God fashioned some souls with gold, some with silver and some with bronze; the souls with gold are to be rulers, those with silver, warriors, the rest of the people being souls with bronze and iron. This is similar to the Rig Vedic myth on the origins of the caste system, which says different groups of people originated from different parts of the body of a primordial being. Those who are supposed to have known the Forms are in a position to create such myths, make propaganda and do many other things as they please, in the name of the general good. In the 20thcentury, Stalin and Mao might as well have thought that they too knew the Forms.

Think on it

1. What kind of communication issues can arise between the one who knows the Truth and others who do not know?
2. What is the relationship between truth and opinion in a democracy?
3. What is a Form?
4. What is Aristotle's criticism of the theory of Forms?
5. Which class of people is expected to know the Forms? And why?
6. What is the myth about the creation of souls that Plato created?
7. What are some of the political implications of the theory of Forms?

CHAPTER FOUR

Democracy and Degeneration of Soul

Plato saw close parallels between the self and the society, or between the soul and the political system. As the political system degenerates, the soul also degenerates and vice versa. Plato thought of the just soul in terms of a hierarchy of certain faculties and desires. At the top is the reason, in the middle are courage and honour, and at the third level desire for physical pleasures, sex, comforts, and money.

To Plato, the ideal society is the one in which reason-dominant people are ruling. The ideal rulers are the philosopher-kings, but if it's the warriors who are ruling then that is the next best, and after that come other political systems.

The philosophers and the warriors put together are called guardians. But sometimes the selection of these guardians can go wrong or they can get corrupted in time. In a system where private property is allowed, desire can become more important than reason, and warfare becomes more important than philosophy, the ideal system degenerates into a timocracy. In the real world, Sparta was ruled by warriors and it was closer to being a timocracy.

A timocracy can further degenerate into an oligarchy when wealth becomes more important than courage and honour, and greed is predominant. Oligarchy can further degenerate into a democracy.

In Plato's scheme, democracy has a very low place. When people start pursuing their passions without any restraint, where there is no hierarchy of desires within a person and no hierarchy of classes in the society, it is democracy.

In a democracy, the base pleasures are pursued without any respect to reason. There is no restraint on comforts and sex. Democracy as a political system corresponds to the soul in which base impulses become dominant and are no more guided by wisdom.

This may be a pertinent observation for our times because it is these kinds of changes that could have given rise to an economic system where Gross Domestic Product becomes the all-important focus of the political system. The pursuit of any pleasure or desire is taken as an expression of liberty and freedom in a democracy.

Traditionally, control over the desire for these lowly pleasures was seen as freedom. In Indian religions such as Hinduism, Buddhism, and Jainism, the word 'maharaja' (the 'great king') or 'jain' has a deeper meaning of conqueror of the desire for base pleasures. But in present-day capitalism and democracy, the pursuit of base pleasures is seen as a sign of liberty or freedom. Plato could envisage a situation like this and considered democracy as a manifestation of the degeneration of the soul.

But democracy is still not the worst form of government, it can further degenerate into tyranny. According to Plato, people in a democracy may choose a leader who begins to oppress the rich and to oppress the rich he will hire men, who will later be used against the people. Then the system becomes a tyranny. This description matches exactly with what happened in the communist regimes of Russia and China in the 20thcentury. In tyranny or despotism, the base passions lead the soul.

In a democracy, the leaders tend to ignite the base passions of people such as hate and envy. Why would they do that? Because they just want to get power somehow. This hate can be directed against another nation or a community within the country. It happens because there is a loss of contact with reason and wisdom.

Communalism, majoritarianism, wars for glory, and rampant materialism – all of it boils down to the souls of people functioning at their lowest level.

The demagogues appeal to the prejudices of the people. The truth becomes a casualty and uninformed opinions become widespread. There is a disconnect between truth and power. When the system is ruled by philosopher-kings, truth and wisdom run the system; but when it is ruled by demagogues, prejudices, hatred, and base emotions run the system.

Plato's criticism of democracy is about a situation where people participate in the government. Many criticise modern democracies on the ground that people are not getting enough participation. There can be excessive centralisation in a modern democracy. Commercial interests may dominate over people's interests. This kind of typical criticism of democracy arises from the fact that people are not participating in the government as they should in a true democracy. But Plato's criticism is different, his problem is with people participating in the government rather than not participating.

When the system degenerates, the good people would not want to be a part of it. When society is corrupt, a just man will not want to take part in it. Plato says: "In accepting power and honours, the just man will be ready to enjoy any position in public or private life which he thinks will make him a better man and avoid any that would break down the established order within him."

In our times, many good people don't run for elections, and even among those who contest, people will choose those who are more popular rather than the best among the candidates. Finally, it turns out that the representatives elected by the people tend to be poor quality humans.

Two hundred years ago, a French thinker De Tocqueville, travelled through America and made observations on the state of democracy there at that time. What he wrote in his book Democracy in America comes very close to Plato's description: "When a democratic man is told that some pleasures should be sought and valued as arising from desires of a higher order, others chastised and enslaved because the desires are base, he will shut the gates of the citadel against the messengers of truth, shaking his head and declaring that one appetite is as good as another and all must have their equal rights." He says further, "His life is subject to no order or restraint, and he has no wish to change an existence which he calls pleasant, free and happy."

Essentially democracy is a system that is not led by wisdom and reason, but by prejudices and mean motives. These ideas of Plato are relevant for our times and are worthy of reflection.

Think on it

1. Who rules an ideal political system?
2. What guides an ideal soul?
3. What is a timocracy?
4. What is the state of a soul corresponding to timocracy?
5. What is the state of a soul corresponding to democracy?
6. What is the traditional religious notion of freedom? What is the modern notion?
7. What are the problems of modern democracy?
8. Why do not good people generally show interest in the running of a democracy?
9. What are De Tocqueville's observations on democracy in America?
10. How relevant are Plato's ideas on democracy?

Aristotle

Aristotle

CHAPTER FIVE

Man as a Political Being

Aristotle (384–322 BCE) was born in Stagira, Greece, to a court physician. That may be one of the reasons why he developed a deep interest in biology and other sciences. His philosophical views tend to be more scientific, and some of his major philosophical ideas have a biological perspective, as we shall see. Aristotle came to Athens to study at Plato's Academy and stayed there for 20 years until Plato's death in 347 BCE. When the Academy was passed over to Plato's nephew, Aristotle left Athens and worked as a tutor to a young Alexander from 343 to 340 BCE.

As Alexander became a king and set out on his mission to conquer the world, Aristotle came back to Athens and found his institute called Lyceum. After Alexander's death, Aristotle faced political problems in Athens and found it prudent to leave the city. He feared meeting the same fate as Socrates. He said he was leaving Athens "lest the Athenians sin against philosophy a second time."

Whereas Socrates decided to stay in Athens at any cost and faced death, Aristotle moved to another place – this also shows the differences in their approaches. Socrates is idealistic and uncompromising, and Plato picked it up from him. But Aristotle is more pragmatic, though he shared the attitude towards some bigger issues with Plato and Socrates, such as the view that ethics and politics should go together. He also thought that knowledge, goodness and happiness go together. Aristotle wrote two books

Nicomachean Ethics and Politics and he felt these works on ethics and politics form one continuous treatise.

Aristotle's political views are far more pragmatic than those of Plato. Aristotle has his own theory of Forms and it helps us understand his approach to politics. How does Aristotle's theory of Forms differ from that of Plato? To Plato, our sensory world is a realm of shadows, only in the world of ideas there is truth which is called Form. A table is a shadow in the sensory world, but a rectangle is its Form. Plato saw the sensory world as consisting of shadows and the objects of the sensory world as "participating" in the Forms. Aristotle rejected this notion.

Aristotle looked at things the way a biologist looks at them. Take a mango seed, it becomes a tree given proper conditions. Aristotle's theory of Forms is based on such a simple fact. Aristotle rejects the idea that there are only shadows in the world we sense and live in, corresponding to the Forms in the ideal world, as Plato said. He postulates that we can see anything in the sensory world in terms of what it is and what it is going to be – its actual and its potential. A seed is an actual thing, but a tree is its potential. A seed represents being, a tree represents the becoming of that seed.

Aristotle says this becoming is there in the being at any time. That is, a seed carries the tree within itself. A tree is immanent in a seed, which means it is there within. To Aristotle, the Forms are not those that exist in the world of ideas, they are simply the potential of the things that exist in the sensory world. A real table can approach towards being a perfect rectangle, not that it is participating in some abstract Form of perfection. To Aristotle, anything that exists as a potential within an object can be actualized. There is no need to posit any abstract world of ideas in which Forms are supposed to exist.

A seed can grow up to be a small tree or a big tree. This potential is empirical. Aristotle went by what is possible and empirical, rather than any abstract notion. Only a mango seed can become a mango tree, a neem seed cannot become a mango tree, it is natural for the mango seed to become a mango tree.

Man's nature

Aristotle examined what is man's nature from the perspective of his theory of Forms. If a tree exists within a seed in a potential form, a man exists in a human embryo in a potential form. It is natural for the embryo to develop in a particular way and eventually become a man.

A man is formed according to the plan of nature just as a tree is formed. What is essential to man is the reason. And he wants to be happy. What makes him happy is goodness. Goodness is not something that comes from some other principles, it is simply what makes a man happy. Happiness and goodness can go together if the proper reason is employed, as Socrates said. And to be like that is natural to man, that's what man is for in nature's scheme of things.

It is natural for man to be good, to be rational, to be happy like it is natural for a seed to finally become a tree and realize itself. Aristotle extends this logic from an individual to associations. A family is a small association, next is a village, next is a political community. To Aristotle, this progression is natural. Man's higher faculties are being expressed when he is moving beyond his family. In a family, a man is primarily meeting his biological needs, but in a political community, the question is of higher-end needs.

The pursuit of freedom is man's nature. Wanting to be happier and freer is man's nature. Like a tree is hidden in the seed, man's political nature exists within him. Man exists as a part of a political community, and that is natural to him.

The possibility of man's political growth, his search to find the truth, his desire to be free, to be good – all of it exists within him as potential. Aristotle thinks of the end and sees that the end is there as a potential in the beginning.

The end and the beginning is one way of looking at things, another way is in terms of whole and part. When the part is taking shape, it knows its place and function, it has an idea of the whole. Similarly, man exists only as a part of a larger political community.

What is a virtue?

Aristotle's theory of Forms is applied to ethics too. A good tree is a real tree, not an imaginary tree of perfection. Similarly, a virtue is a real thing and not an imaginary idea of perfection. People have an idea of what qualities make a good man, and those qualities become virtues when they are seen in real men.

Aristotle also asserts that virtue is the "mean" between two vices. The virtue of courage lies between cowardice and foolhardiness, two vices. His main point is that goodness lies somewhere between two bad things. Both the bad things are real, and the good thing is also real.

Think on it

1. What do you know about Aristotle's education?
2. What institute did Aristotle set up and when?
3. How is Aristotle's theory of Forms different from that of Plato?
4. How is becoming a part of being?
5. What is the relationship between being and becoming?
6. Why is forming a political community natural to men?
7. What is the continuity between Socrates and Aristotle?
8. Is man by nature political?
9. How does Aristotle see a virtue?

CHAPTER SIX

Polity: the Best Form of Government

Aristotle sees a political community as something natural – as natural as a tree or an animal. "It is evident that the *polis* belongs to the class of things that exist by nature and that man is by nature a political animal." What does Aristotle mean by political animal? Man's reasoning, his freedom-seeking tendencies, his decision-making capabilities, and his social being – all of these exist in a political context. "He who is without a *polis*, by reason of his own nature and not of some accident, is either a poor sort of being, or a being higher than man."

Aristotle considers the mature stage of any changing and growing thing as the actualizing of its natural potential. "If the art of shipbuilding were in the wood [instead of being in an artist], it would act like nature; hence, if art proceeds to some end, so does nature."

The aim of a political community is to promote goodness. "A state exists for the sake of a good life, and not for the sake of life only: if life only were the object, slaves and brute animals might form a state, but they cannot, for they have no share in happiness or in a life of free choice."

Out of man's search for freedom, a state is formed. "Every state is a community of some kind, and every community is established with a view to some good; for mankind always acts in order to obtain that which they think good. But, if all communities aim at some good, the state or political community, which is the highest of all, and which embraces all the rest, aims at a good in a greater degree than any other, and at the highest good."

Types of political systems

A state can be described in terms of its constitution. "Constitution of a state is in a sense the way it lives." "When the constitution undergoes a change in form and becomes a different constitution, the city will likewise cease to be the same city. We say that a chorus which appears at one time as a comic and at another as a tragic chorus is not the same – and this in spite of the fact that the members often remain the same."

Aristotle collected 158 written constitutions and he classified them into six types of governments. Monarchy is where there is only one ruler. In an aristocracy, there are a few rulers. In what Aristotle called polity, many people rule. With each of these three types, Aristotle says, there are corresponding bad forms. Monarchy is good when the ruler is a philosopher-king, but it devolves into tyranny when the ruler is bad. Aristocracy is good but oligarchy is bad. Polity is good but democracy is bad.

The word 'democracy' is being used in a negative sense by Aristotle, the same way Plato used it. Oligarchs are rich people who are good at making money but not at reasoning. "Some think that if they are superior in one point, for example in wealth, they are superior in all." And democracy goes by "arithmetic justice." Those who believe in democracy "believe that if they are equal, in one respect, for instance in free birth, they are equal all round." These ways of thinking are wrong.

Aristotle sees virtue as something that lies between two vices, and he does the same thing for a political system too. To him, a good political system is something that lies between oligarchy and democracy, being a mix of them. A democracy can be good, it can be a 'polity' if it is run within a proper framework of the law.

Aristotle gives great importance to the rule of law. "He who bids the law rule may be deemed to bid God and Reason alone rule, but he bids man rule adds an element of the beast; for desire is a wild beast, and passion perverts the minds of rulers, even when they are the best of men. The law is reason unaffected by desire." This position contrasts with that of Plato who once argued that a wise ruler should not be constrained by laws. Plato however changed his view in his later works.

Oligarchy plus democracy would amount to a mixed constitution. Aristotle arrives at the value of this mixed constitution in the same way he arrives at anything good and virtuous. "We have now to consider what is the best constitution and the best way of life for the majority of cities and the majority of mankind. In doing so, we shall not employ a standard of excellence above the reach of ordinary people, or a standard of education requiring exceptional natural endowments and equipment, or the standard of a constitution which attains an ideal level. We shall be concerned only with the sort of life which most people are able to share and the sort of constitutions which it is possible for most cities to enjoy."

"Both oligarchy and democracy may be tolerable forms of government, even though they deviate from the ideal. But if you push either of the further still [in the direction to which it tends], you will begin by making it a worse constitution, and you may end up turning it into something which is not a constitution at all. The nearest to the best must always be better, and the one farthest removed from the mean must always be worse."

A polity, which is a mixed form of democracy and oligarchy, has predominant middle classes. In a democracy, poor people dominate and go by their class interests. In an oligarchy, the rich go by their interests. Aristotle wants the mean, a society dominated neither by the rich nor the poor. So there should be enough people who belong to the middle class. Aristotle is using his theory of the mean to identify middle classes as preferable. "It is, therefore, the greatest of blessings for a city that its members should possess a moderate and adequate property. Where some have great possessions, and others have nothing at all, the result is either extreme democracy or an unmixed oligarchy; or it may even be, as a result of the excesses of both sides, a tyranny."

"A city aims at being, as far as possible, composed of equals and peers, which is the condition of those in the middle, more than any other group. It follows that this kind of city is bound to have the best constitution since it is composed of the elements which, in our view, naturally go to make up a city." Class conflict emerges when the power is completely either with the rich or with the poor. Aristotle's observations on the importance of the middle class for the stability of a political system has indeed been vindicated by modern history.

Conservative thinking

Aristotle thinks in terms of a mean for everything. And he thinks only in terms of available alternatives. The problem with this approach is that he can't see all the human possibilities. A bunch of seeds give rise to a few average-size trees, but under a different set of conditions, some of these seeds could give rise to huge trees. Aristotle is missing the possibility of the big trees. The same logic can be applied to political systems also.

Aristotle rightly rejects the communism of family. "What is common to the greatest number gets the least amount of care. People pay most attention to what is their own; they care less for what is common. People are more prone to neglect their duty when they think that another is attending to it." "Just as a little sweet wine, mixed with a great deal of water, produces a tasteless mixture, so the family feeling is diluted and tasteless when family names have as little meaning as they have in a constitution of this sort, and when there is so little reason for a father treating his sons as sons, or a son treating his father as a father, or brothers one another as brothers."

But his position on women is indefensible. "We should look upon the female state as being as it were a deformity, though one which occurs in the ordinary course of nature." How can what occurs in the ordinary course of nature be seen as a deformity? "A male is male in virtue of a particular ability, and a female female in virtue of a particular inability." In Sparta, women were taking part in war in those days. Nor was he influenced on this by Plato who thought women could be rulers.

Aristotle's attitude towards slavery is similarly very demeaning. "All men who differ from others as much as the body differs from the soul or an animal from man (and in this case with all whose function is bodily service, and who produce best when they supply such service) – all such are by nature slaves." "The slave is entirely without the faculty of deliberation; the female indeed possess it, but in a form which lacks authority; and children also possess it, but only in an immature form."

Aristotle was making these observations when people defeated in wars were being turned into slaves. There was even a time when the Athenians feared they could be taken as slaves, though fortunately, it did not happen. So sometimes even philosophers could be turned into slaves.

It may be true that some people don't make efforts to apply their higher faculties and so might appear as slaves by nature. Had Aristotle taken that position, calling the people who fail to use their intelligence slaves, it would have made sense. But Aristotle did not bother to clarify that the people who may be working as slaves might not be slaves by nature.

Aristotle found slavery and he justified it. He found patriarchy and he justified it. He didn't see the potential alternatives to the existing things. He had a very conservative attitude in many things. This is a serious limitation of his thought. May be rooted in his theory of virtue, which he takes as a mean between the vices and empirically existing.

Think on it

1. How is a man by nature political?
2. How is a political community natural?
3. What is a constitution to a political community?
4. Explain the six types of political systems.
5. What is a mixed constitution that Aristotle prefers?
6. What is Aristotle's attitude towards women?
7. What is Aristotle's position on slaves?

St.Augustine

St. Augustine

CHAPTER SEVEN

Should a State Help People Overcome the Original Sin?

St. Augustine (354–430) was a medieval political thinker whose philosophy was derived from Christianity. He was born to a Christian mother and a pagan father. Paganism was an important belief at that time. He was converted to Christianity at the age of 32. Around that time, 381 CE, Christianity became the state religion of the Roman empire. Earlier, Augustine belonged to a sect called Manichaeanism, which taught that good and evil are coequal, unlike Christianity which considers good to be superior. He also came into contact with Platonic and neo-Platonic ideas. His major political work is The City of God, which he wrote when he was the bishop of Hippo, a city in North Africa. He wrote it in response to those who said Rome was lost to the barbarians because of its new religion, i.e., Christianity.

Augustine lived in the last stage of the Roman empire. His political views were influenced by the existing Christian doctrine. He makes certain assumptions on the nature of man and puts forth a political system based on them.

In his autobiographical work Confessions, Augustine describes an incident that revealed to him what is human nature. The incident deals with stealing. When he was a child, he stole pears. He says it was not because he wanted pears, but because he wanted to steal because stealing is evil. He observes that he derived pleasure not from what he stole, but from the fact of doing something forbidden. He was shocked why it was like that.

As a proverb says, stolen fruits are sweeter. That's what Augustine was experiencing. What is the source of this pleasure of stealing? What aspect of human nature does this pleasure reveal?

He says the pleasure from stealing came from what is called the original sin. In Christianity, the original sin refers to the story of Adam and Eve eating the forbidden fruit when prompted by the devil who came in the form of a serpent. After they ate this fruit, they lost their innocence and were thrown out of the Garden of Eden. Augustine writes: "So great a sin was committed, that by it human nature was altered for the worse, and was transmitted also to their posterity."

The man was created good by God. Then the original sin by Adam and Eve transmitted the propensity to sin to all. This means that the desire to do evil is there in everyone. Augustine says: "I loved my own perdition and my own faults, not the things for which I committed wrong, but wrong itself. The evil in me was foul, but I loved it."

The desire to commit evil is a part of human nature. "If babies are innocent, it is not for lack of will to do harm, but for lack of strength." Babies are born with evil. Evil is not a result of the socialisation process. Still, there are good people too. "But some are saved by the grace of God – though not completely and forever."

People are born with differences in terms of good and bad. From this understanding of human nature, Augustine proposes a political arrangement. People are basically of two types but all of them live together. Both kinds of people want order and peace. Some want to pursue their own self, and some want to pursue God. And because everyone wants order and peace, both these types of people accept a state. Augustine is not very different from Hobbes and Freud in having these views, except that he clothes them in religious terms.

Augustine says good people and bad people belong to two different cities: "Two cities have been formed by two loves: the earthly by the love of self, even to the contempt of God; the heavenly by the love of God, even to the contempt of self. In the one, the princes and the nations it subdues are ruled by the love of ruling; in the other, the princes and the subjects serve one another in love, the latter obeying, while the former take thought for all."

Those who love their own selves want peace so that they can obtain the pleasures of the self, and those who love God want peace so that they can contemplate on God. Both need a state. They need law. "Whether they love self or God, all require peace." Then he says: "All authority including that of the state is derived from God. So man should obey unless the laws are sinful." This is called a theocratic view of the state.

Augustine says that the work of the state is not so important. It is not for any ethical purpose. "As far as this life of mortals is concerned, which is spent and ended in a few days, what does it matter under whose government a dying man lives." Why only a few days? Augustine sees beyond this life on earth. He thinks of the other world. "What does it matter under whose government a dying man lives?"

Augustine doesn't think highly of any state. "Without justice, what are kingdoms but great robberies?" What is a state? Just a robbery. "As a pirate asks Alexander in the Cicero's commonwealth, 'What I do with a petty ship, you do with a fleet. I am a robber, you are emperor.'"

When people were complaining that the Roman empire collapsed and it was such a great empire, Augustine wrote, "What is that empire? They talk about justice, but really there is no justice." He says, "Look at the naked deeds: weigh them naked, judge them naked."

This kind of analysis came to be known as realpolitik, which means thinking in terms of what a state is and not what it should be. The word 'realpolitik' came from Augustine. One can agree with the concept of the original sin but still differ with Augustine when one says that the state should help man in getting his salvation.

Think on it

1. What is the context of St. Augustine's work?
2. What is the concept of original sin?
3. What is Augustine's view of human nature?
4. Why are some people good?
5. Why do both good people and bad people want state?
6. What is a state meant for?
7. Is there justice in the state?

Machiavelli

Machiavelli

CHAPTER EIGHT

Reflections: Can a Teacher Tell His Students 'Be Corrupt'?

I teach the Ethics course, and in this course, I sometimes tell my students, “Do not mind to lie, cheat, and deceive when needed or to be corrupt if needed.” The subject of Ethics is meant to make the students ethically more sound, whereas I am saying “Be bad.” Why do I do this?

I find that many students want to do good things, want to serve society, but they also have a very rigid idea of what is good and bad. They want to be good, they want to serve society, and they think it is difficult to be both. They think that society is for bad people, and how can one be good in this bad society? When I ask them what is meant by being good, their idea of being good is that they should follow the law, they should follow the rules, and they should be good as per what the parents said about being good.

I believe once some of them enter the service they soon find that they are not able to be good. They feel disappointed and resigned to the situation and participate in doing they do not like. This happens because they don’t question what is truly good, why they think something is good or why something came to be called good. There is no independent reasoning. They go by what their parents told them and what the newspapers tell. What I want is that before wanting to be good, they should explore what is good and why something is called good.

One should go for conscious ethical reasoning. I would say such reasoning is what the aim of the subject is. It is in that context I question how society's moral code has evolved and whether it is right. For example, lying; you don't want to reveal something, but the other person, insists you do so. What option do you have other than lying? You should lie. If you don't want to lie, you are granting him the right to information about you.

'Not to lie under any circumstances cannot, therefore, be a part of a moral code. Similar is the case with keeping promises. Someone comes to you with a particular proposal and both of you agree upon it. He is getting you into this fully knowing he will not follow but you will follow because you believe in honesty! In such a situation, you may lose. I expect you to understand this game and be prepared not to honour your word under certain circumstances.

I want the students to think that life is very vast. Life is, I would say, in the end, a mystery. You can't follow a particular code across all situations. A particular code you socialised into may have been a way of controlling you. I want the students to find out for themselves what is good rather than follow what is good as told by the society – be its laws or be its religion. I want the students to have an experimental attitude towards life.

Never think that you should rigorously follow the conventional moral code – according to which you should be honest, you should be good, you should be a person of integrity and all those things. Instead, be prepared to be dishonest, be prepared to be bad because sometimes that too could be needed. Reflect on what you want, what are the ends you are seeking, what are the means and why the moral code is like this.

One may wonder, what kind of people are the students going to be if taught this way? I think they will be more intelligent. I think in the end, they come out to be better citizens.

Even with children, I prefer this questioning approach. Often the parents use the words 'good' and 'bad' to control the children. 'Good boy' drinks milk at 7:30 AM everyday! A 'good boy' sleeps by

10 PM. A 'good boy' always goes by what his mother says. A lot of violence is being perpetrated on the children in the name of 'good boy', and 'good girl'. I sometimes ask the children: "Why do you want to be always good, can't you be bad? When are you going to be bad?"

Once I found my son who was in 5thclass just outside the home, on the other side of the road, on a cycle but unwilling to cross the road. I asked him "What are you waiting for?" He said, "Mother asked me not to cross the road till she comes." And he was just standing there.

Years later, when he got admission to an engineering college, we went with him. On the orientation day, the authorities gave him a list of rules: not to use the phone at particular times, not to use a camera phone, and all kinds of such things. He read them and he was so much worried. "If I have to follow all of them, what is my life going to be here?" Then I told him very clearly, "Remember for life, whatever rule there is, it is meant to be broken under certain circumstances. That is the first point about rules. Then, will you not be punished? Find it out. There are certain rules which are not meant to be followed at all. There are rules which they insist should be followed. Also, see what are the punishments that they are giving and whether the risk of punishment less than what you would gain by not following it."

"Don't internalise these rules. If you are violating them, don't think you are becoming a bad boy." This is what I told him. Otherwise, he would be frightened by the rules.

The world is like a game between opposing forces. If a police officer wants to follow all the rules, and a rowdy has no rules, who will win? The officer has to think about it. How do we know that those rules are good? How do we know that the moral code is correct? When do we say something is good? This is the kind of reasoning that should be inculcated even in the children.

The Prince

A ruler of a principality, that is, a prince, should know very clearly that if he follows the general moral code rigidly if he chooses to be good as per the conventional moral code, it would be self-destruction. It is in this spirit Machiavelli wrote The Prince.

Machiavelli lived from 1469 to 1527, in Italy. He entered the service of the Florentine republic in 1498. He observed the highest layers of governance from close quarters, and not only of the Florentine republic but of other places too because he was a diplomat and had contacts with the top officials, the rulers, and religious authorities in Italy and outside. A coup took place in 1512 and he lost his job because he was accused of having a role in it. He was arrested and tortured in 1513 for his alleged conspiracy against the Medici, the new rulers who destroyed the republic.

Soon thereafter Machiavelli started writing The Prince and completed it by the end of 1513. The Prince was a kind of job application to potential employers. It was advice on how a ruler should behave. In the subsequent years, Machiavelli also wrote Discourses on Livy (1513-17), which was a series of books, Art of War (1521) and Florentine History (1525).

Machiavelli wanted to say what a king should be. He said many things which people then and even now find outrageous. The word 'Machiavellian' has come to refer to somebody cunning and mean. But when I read The Prince, I didn't feel that way. It seemed closer to my Ethics classes where I tell my students, "Be bad if need be."

My viewpoint is just his viewpoint also: "Many have dreamed up republics and principalities which have never in truth been known to exist; the gulf between how one should live and how one does live is so wide that a man who neglects what is actually done for what should be done moves towards self-destruction rather than self-preservation. The fact is that a man who wants to act virtuously in every way necessarily comes to grief among so many who are not virtuous. Therefore, if a prince wants to maintain his rule he must be prepared not to be virtuous and to make use of this or not according to need" (Chapter 15).

This is exactly my concern. I feel my students have a preconceived notion of what the administration is, which is not actually what it is. They want to handle it being virtuous in a conventional sense. But I believe they should be prepared not to be virtuous.

Machiavelli goes on to say: "Taking everything into consideration, he will find that some of the things that appear to be virtues will, if he practices them, ruin him, and some of the things that appear to be vices will bring him security and prosperity."

These are universal truths – neither time-specific nor culture-specific – and are useful for intelligent living.

Think on it

1. Is refusing to lie under all circumstances be a good thing?
2. Why is ethical reasoning important?
3. Can a rigid moral code remove flexibility in responding to a situation?
4. How can a wrong moral code contribute to failure and unhappiness?
5. What do you know about Machiavelli?
6. What is the context of The Prince?
7. Was The Prince relevant only in Machiavelli's time?

CHAPTER NINE

Whom Should a Prince Emulate? Rama or Krishna?

Let's discuss Machiavelli in terms of two gods we are familiar with, Rama and Krishna. Rama is a very straightforward person, who always honours his word. Krishna does all kinds of things, he lies, he cheats, deceives, but in the end, delivers justice. He doesn't seem to go by any moral code that others follow. However, he seems to have his own moral code that is informed by justice and compassion.

Of course, we ordinary humans cannot be like Krishna because if we do things the way Krishna does, we may be caught while deceiving and be punished. Krishna being a god has control over things. In the end, he delivers justice and is not caught in between.

Rama is extremely rule-oriented. Once he gives his word, he will follow it, even if the circumstances don't warrant it. His father made a promise to one of his wives long ago, and to let him honour that word Rama went to live in the forest. If Krishna was placed in a similar situation, he would have ways to get around it.

These are two models that the Indian tradition offers. Machiavelli is very clearly for Krishna, though we can't say that the higher justice that Krishna delivers is something that Machiavelli too wants.

Machiavelli is not calling for an unjust state. He too wants to promote order and justice, but he is concerned that a particular understanding of a moral code should not tie up a king and make him like Rama. In Satya Harischandra, we have an even worse example of what happens to somebody if he honours his word rigidly. He ends up losing his kingdom, property and family.

Not honouring words

Machiavelli says many successful rulers dishonoured their word when they thought it was right to do so. "The princes who have achieved great things have been those who have given their word lightly, who have known how to trick men with their cunning, and who, in the end, have overcome those abiding by honest principles."

"A prudent ruler cannot, must not, honour his word when it places him at a disadvantage and when the reasons for which he made his promise no longer exist. Because men are wretched creatures who would not keep their word to you, you need not keep your word to them" (Chapter 18).

Being a miser

Sometimes what appears to be a virtue, like generosity, may not be a virtue at all. "Because a prince can't practice the virtue of generosity in such a way that he is noted for it, except to his cost, he should if he is prudent not mind being called a miser."

But he is not really a miser. "In time he will be recognised as being essentially a generous man seeing that because of his parsimony his existing revenues are enough for him, he can defend himself against an aggressor, and he can embark on campaign without burdening the people" (Ch. 16).

To be feared

"It is far better to be feared than loved if you cannot be both. For love is secured by a bond of gratitude which men, wretched creatures that they are, break when it is to their advantage to do so; but fear is strengthened by a dread of punishment which is always effective."

A prince should not be hated by his people. "The prince must none the less make himself feared in such a way that, if he is not loved, at least he escapes being hated. For fear is quire compatible with an absence of hatred" (Ch. 17).

"He will be hated if he is rapacious and aggressive with regard to the property and the women of his subjects" (Ch. 19).

Machiavelli says: "One man should not be afraid of improving his possession, lest they be taken away from him, or another deterred by high taxes from starting a new business" (Ch. 21).

Machiavelli links hatred engendered against a ruler with the instability of his regime: "One of the most powerful safeguards a prince can have against conspiracies is to avoid being hated by the populace. This is because the conspirator always thinks that by killing the prince he will satisfy the people, but if he thinks that he will outrage the people, he will never have the courage to go ahead with his enterprise" (Ch.19).

He says: "When the prince has a goodwill of the people he must not worry about conspirators; but when the people are hostile and regard him with hatred he must go in fear of everything and everyone" (Ch. 19).

What do people want? Security of property and their women. There should be peace. No high taxation. When the prince dies, the people should not feel happy. Machiavelli is not advising the prince to enjoy the power and do whatever he can do with it. He wants the ruler to think about the purpose of power and know that his success is linked to the well-being of the people. This amounts to good advice. Machiavelli is proposing a moral code that makes such a rule possible. He is talking about what traits the king should have and why he should have them.

Law not enough

Machiavelli says that law alone is not enough to maintain power. "There are two ways of fighting: by law or by force. The first way is natural to men and the second to beasts. But as the first way often proves inadequate, one needs to have recourse to the second. So a prince must understand how to make nice use of the beast and the man."

"A prince is forced to know how to act like a beast, he must learn from the fox and the lion; because the lion is defenceless against traps and a fox is defenceless against wolves" (Ch 18). A prince can't bank only on the law, only on strength and he should be willing to play games.

Appearances matter

"He should appear to be compassionate, faithful to his word, kind, guileless and devout. And indeed, he should be so. But his disposition should be such that, if he needs to be the opposite, he knows how" (Ch. 18). Machiavelli is not saying that a prince should not have the qualities known as virtues, but he can't be bound by them.

New prince

"A prince, and especially a new prince, can not observe all those things which give a man a reputation for virtue. He should have a flexible disposition, varying as fortune and circumstances dictate" (Ch. 18).

A new prince usually faces a dynamic situation. The problem with any moral code is that it is for a static situation. A new prince would be dealing with many unusual things. In an established principality, it may be easier to follow the moral code, but in a new one, it will be more difficult.

"He should not deviate from what is good if that is possible, but he should know how to do evil if that is necessary" (Ch. 18).

"A certain contemporary ruler never preaches anything except peace and good faith, and he is an enemy of both one and the other, and if he had ever honoured either of them he would have lost either his standing or his state many times over" (Ch. 18)

Empiricism

Machiavelli reinforces his standpoint with examples from history. Arguing how fear is more important than love, in case there is a conflict between them, he says, "Among the admirable achievements of Hannibal is included this: that although he led a huge army, made up of countless different races, on foreign campaigns, there was never any dissension. For this, his inhuman cruelty is wholly responsible. If it had not been for his cruelty, his other qualities would not have been enough. The historians, having given little thought to this, on the one hand, admire what Hannibal achieved, and on the other condemn what made his achievement possible" (Ch 17). Machiavelli's method is comparative, historical and empirical. The Prince is full of examples like that of Hannibal here.

Harmful good deeds

Don't think that goodness automatically contributes to power, it need not. Sometimes even good deeds can be hated. "It should be noted one can be hated just as much for good deeds as for evil ones. Whenever that class of men on which you believe your continued rule depends is corrupt, whether it be the populace, or soldiers, or nobles, you have to satisfy it by adopting the same disposition; and then good deeds are your enemies" (Ch. 19).

Not too much criticism

Machiavelli advises on what type of advisors a prince should have. "The only way to safeguard yourself against flatterers is by letting people understand that you are not offended by the truth, but if everyone can speak the truth to you then you lose respect. A shrewd policy should adopt a middle way, choosing wise men for his government and allowing only those the freedom to speak the truth to him, and then only concerning matters on which he asks their opinion, and nothing else" (Ch. 23).

On assassins

"It should be noted that princes cannot escape death if the attempt is made by a fanatic, because anyone who has no fear of death himself can succeed in inflicting it. The prince should restrain himself from inflicting grave injury on anyone in his service whom he has close to him in his affairs of state" (Ch. 19). After Operation Blue Star, Indira Gandhi was advised to remove her Sikh security guards from her home. She refused. She didn't see that their community was badly hurt, and they might avenge!

Role of fortune

If one follows all these principles, can one be successful? "I believe that it is probably true that fortune is the arbiter of half the things we do, leaving the other half or so to be controlled by ourselves." By "fortune" he meant changing circumstances. "As fortune is changeable whereas men are obstinate in their ways, men prosper so long as fortune and policy are in accord, and when there is a clash, they fail" (Ch. 25).

A prince can always respond wisely to the changed circumstances. "God does not want to do everything Himself and take away from us our free will and our share of the glory which belongs to us." (Ch. 26).

Use of religion

Machiavelli discussed the relevance of religion in The Discourses. "The observance of divine institutions is the cause of the greatness of republics. The disregard of them produces their ruin; for where the fear of God is wanting, there the country will come to ruin unless it is sustained by the fear of the prince, which may temporarily supply the want of religion. But as the lives of princes are short, the kingdom will of necessity perish as the prince fails in virtue." Machiavelli's would agree with Voltaire's statement, "If God did not exist, it would be necessary to invent him."

Religion should teach the right things, but Machiavelli was sure that Christianity was not doing that. Christian principles "have made men feeble and caused them to become an easy prey to evil-minded men, who can control them more securely, seeing that the great body of men, for the sake of gaining Paradise, are more disposed to endure injuries than to avenge them." This is the same as Nietzsche's position on Christianity.

Like Nietzsche would some centuries later, Machiavelli preferred the pagan religion of antiquity to Christianity, as it "deified only men who had achieved great glory, such as commanders of armies and chiefs of republics, whilst ours glorifies more the humble and contemplative men than the men of action."

Think on it

1. What does Machiavelli say about honouring one's promises?
2. What does Machiavelli say about a ruler being hated by his people?
3. Should a ruler be feared or loved?
4. Why should a prince be like a fox?
5. Why should a prince appear to be good?
6. Why should a new prince be more careful?
7. How is Machiavelli's approach scientific?
8. What kind of advisors should a prince hire?
9. Who can turn into the assassin of a ruler?
10. How should a prince make use of changed circumstances?
11. How is religion useful to a prince?

Hobbes

Thomas Hobbes

CHAPTER TEN

Does Darwinism Agree With Hobbes' State of Nature?

Thomas Hobbes (1588–1679) attempted to create a scientific theory of politics. He was acquainted with Galileo and Descartes, he was inspired by the scientific method, particularly that of Galileo. He wanted to derive a political theory from the basics of science. He was influenced by the methods of physics and geometry, and he thought that he should scientifically arrive at what is human nature. From this human nature, he thought he should arrive at the role of the state.

Hobbes tried to think in terms of the body, motion, and some movements in the brain. He thought he analytically derived human nature. Like Galileo discarded Aristotle's science, Hobbes thought he would discard Aristotle's politics.

At that time there was a civil war going on between the Royalists and the Puritans in England. Hobbes was on the side of the royals. During Cromwell's rule, he fled to France and worked as a mathematics tutor to the future king Charles II. He wrote his major work Leviathan in 1651. Though Hobbes was politically on the side of the Royalists, his reasons for supporting the king were different from those of the Royalists. They believed that the king had a divine right to rule, but Hobbes rejected it.

Hobbes tried to build a theory of politics from the basics of physics and mathematics, without reference to any God. Since he did not accept the divine origin of kings, he was banished from Charles' court after his book was published.

State of nature

Through a process of scientific reasoning, Hobbes arrives at the conclusion that man is power-seeking and always desiring something. This power-seeking leads to endless conflict among people, which he calls the "state of nature." Since the state of nature is intolerable, people give their power to a sovereign whose duty is to provide safety to all. This is the social contract theory of Hobbes that explains the source of power of a sovereign as well as its obligation.

"I put for a general inclination of all mankind, a perpetual and restless desire of power after power, that ceases only in death. And the cause of this is not always that a man hopes for a more intensive delight, than he has already attained to; or that he can't be content with a moderate power; but because he cannot assure the power and means to live well, which he has present, without the acquisition of more."

Man seeks power, more power, more and more power. Why so much more power? Because he cannot be sure of retaining the power he has unless he gets more power. This happens to be a key concept in IR school of Realism too.

"The object of man's desire is not to enjoy once only, and for one instant of time; but to assure forever, the way of his future desire."

"The desires and other passions of man are in themselves no sin." Hobbes is rejecting the outlook of the Christian religion.

"Neither is the freedom of willing or not willing greater in man than in other living creatures." Man is not free not to have these desires.

You think Hobbes is exaggerating? He says, "What opinion he has of his fellow subjects, when he rides armed; of his fellow citizens, when he locks his doors; and of his children and servants, when he locks his chests. Does he not there as much accuse mankind by his actions, as I do by my words?"

Hobbes describes the state of nature as follows: "In such condition, there is no place for industry; because the fruit thereof is uncertain: and consequently no culture of the earth; no navigation, nor use of the commodities that may be imported by sea; no account of time; no arts; no letters; no society; and which is worst of all, continual fear and danger of violent death; and the life of man, solitary, poor, nasty, brutish and short."

Is man brutish?

Is Hobbes' understanding of man and the state of nature correct? It seems to be very distorted. There are brutish elements in man, but there are also noble and cooperative elements. Man is both brutish and cooperative by nature. How can one assume that he was originally only brutish?

Moreover, where was this man who was always ready to fight with others? Hobbes does not say that the state of nature is a historical event. And if it is a thought experiment, how valid is it?

Cooperative groups exist even among the animals. Humans are born into cooperative groups, they are born into societies. A species cannot survive without being cooperative. There never were solely brutish men at any time. Man has been brutish as well as cooperative. That's how evolution could take place.

In these cooperative groups, some could even be willing to give their life for others in defending that group. People could have that degree of altruism. Human evolution would not have been possible, even the survival of a species may not be possible, without any cooperation and a degree of sacrifice for others.

Human ancestors lived in groups, and as groups, they evolved into humans. Humans did not emerge at once, they evolved over a very long period. Hobbes wrote Leviathan in 1650, and Darwin came around 200 years later. From Darwin, we learnt that cooperation is essential for the survival of a species, and if everybody is a brute, a population cannot continue. If every life form is against every other life form even in the same species, a community is not possible. Animals cooperate among themselves to live together. They fight as a group against others, which calls for cooperation. They do fight among themselves over scarce resources.

If man was only brutish, the state would not be able to control the people. To control man simply through power is not possible. Man is born into a certain social structure, there is a restraint, there is a process of socialization, all this had been there even before the state emerged. Societies existed much before the state. Hobbes' narrative on how man came to be controlled is wrong – both logically and empirically.

Just observing animal behaviour could have made Hobbes think differently, even without having any idea of human evolution.

Think on it

1. Was Galileo an inspiration to Hobbes? Explain.
2. What was the political context of Hobbes' thought?
3. What is the social contract by which a king rules?
4. What is the "state of nature" according to Hobbes?
5. Is not man naturally cooperative?
6. Does every animal fight with every other animal, even in the same species?
7. What is the difference between society and state?
8. Is Hobbes' account of how the state emerged historically true?
9. How has human nature been controlled in societies?
10. How is Darwinism useful in evaluating Hobbes' theory?

CHAPTER ELEVEN

Hobbes for an Absolutist State

Hobbes believed that the state of nature – every man against every man – is intolerable. Therefore people surrender themselves to a central authority. They will make the central authority very powerful. Hobbes says that the social contract is not made between every man and a central authority, it is made among men themselves. Based on the consent of the people, a central authority is given the powers to rule them, it has no divine right to rule.

Hobbes' theory of sovereignty is this. "Everyone says to every other man: 'I authorize and give up my right of governing myself, to this man, or this assembly of men, on this condition, that you give up your right to him and authorize all his actions in like manner, and he is called SOVEREIGN.'"

A central authority doesn't need to be a person, it can even be an assembly. Hobbes is not referring to a form of government. To a sovereign, all powers are given. The cover page of Leviathan shows an all-powerful sovereign – a king who holds a sword in one hand and the sceptre of the church in the other. This sovereign is made of people, his body is shown as consisting of people.

Hobbes thought that this kind of concentration of power is required to bring peace to society. People must confer "all their power and strength upon one man, or upon one assembly of men, that may reduce all their wills unto one will."

The final authority should rest with the sovereign. Some thinkers claimed that the church should have final authority, but Hobbes didn't agree. The Protestants and the Puritans said that the individual conscience should be the final authority. Hobbes did not think so. He believed that order is not possible without the application of force, which is the task of the sovereign. He said, "Law is a command. Covenants without the sword are but words, and of no strength to secure a man at all."

Hobbes places certain obligations on the sovereign. "The office of the sovereign consists in the end for which he was trusted with sovereign power, namely the procuration of the safety of the people. But by safety here is not meant a bare preservation, but also all other contentments of life, which every man by lawful industry, without danger or hurt to the commonwealth shall acquire to himself."

"The obligation of the subjects to the sovereign is understood to last as long and no longer than the power lasts by which he is able to protect them."

Negative state

Leviathan also says that people have certain liberties that they don't have to give away to the central authority. People should have the liberty "to buy and sell and otherwise contract with one another; to choose their own abode, their own diet, their own trade of life, and institute their children as they themselves think fit; and the like."

People should have the liberty to do these things, and the sovereign need not interfere. This is the concept of a negative state. One can say that Hobbes contributed to the founding of the liberal theory of a negative state. It is this concept that Locke would elaborate upon later, developing a full-fledged theory of the negative state.

Liberal democracies have a separation of powers, but Hobbes rejected the concept of separation of powers. "If there had not first been an opinion received of the greatest part of England that these powers were divided between the King and the Lords and House of Commons, the people had never been divided and fallen into this Civil War." If there was no separation of powers between the Parliament and the sovereign, the civil war would not have happened.

Hobbes spoke for the concentration of powers in a sovereign, that is, for an absolutist state.

Think on it

1. Who is a sovereign?
2. Why was the sovereign made all-powerful?
3. What is the nature of the contract among the citizens of a state?
4. What is meant by a negative state?
5. Did Hobbes have an idea of a negative state?
6. Why did Hobbes reject the idea of separation of powers?

Locke

John Locke

CHAPTER TWELVE

The Idea of a Negative State

John Locke (1632–1704) was a very influential political thinker and is regarded as the father of modern liberal democracy. His major political work is The Second Treatise of Government. It could be difficult to realize the importance of John Locke just because we live with the institutions that were shaped by his ideas, we live in what can be called a Lockean state. Like fish cannot understand what it is to live outside water, we can't understand what it is to live without following Locke's ideas.

The most important idea of Locke is the separation of society and the state. Locke proposed that only a few powers be given to the state, and the society keeps many liberties with itself. The state cannot take them away. This is the concept of the negative state – 'state' meaning the government and all its institutions.

The state is not supposed to take away certain rights of its citizens. In the Indian context, they are called fundamental rights. The Supreme Court can intervene if these rights are violated. Ambedkar calls Article 32 "the heart and soul" of the Constitution because it protects the fundamental rights of Indian citizens. This is an essential feature of liberal democracy. There are certain things the state cannot do if those things violate these rights, however good its intentions are. This is the spirit of liberal democracy.

The state is also regulated through a separation of powers. The executive does not have any legislative power. The separation of the legislature from the executive reduces the power of the executive.

In Locke's view, the legislature represents the will of the people. The legislature is to be periodically elected. The executive should be responsible to the legislature. These features of a democracy that we take for granted are all Locke's ideas.

In certain emergencies, Locke thought that the executive should have prerogative power. It is "the power to act according to discretion, for the public good, without the prescription of the law and sometimes even against it." That is why the Indian Constitution has emergency provisions.

Differences with Hobbes and Filmer

Hobbes thought that society should give all powers to the monarch or an assembly. Otherwise, men would be fighting among themselves because they are power-hungry. Locke said when people are power-hungry and we concentrate the powers in the king or the assembly, they would abuse the power. He said, "Absolute monarchs are but men."

Although Locke seems to counter Hobbes, he had another lesser-known political thinker Robert Filmer in mind rather than Hobbes. Filmer wrote the book "Patriarcha or The Natural Power of Kings" (posthumously published in 1680), defending the absolute power of kings. He defended their divine right to rule, and he did so based on the religious scriptures. Locke's First Treatise of Government has many biblical references because he was arguing against the divine basis for kingship.

Filmer also said that a king is like a father to his people, the king's power is paternal. The king's position belongs to him, like property, and he can pass it on to his heir. This is the traditional view of kingship, and Filmer defended it.

Locke says paternal power does nothing but "flatter the natural vanity and ambition of men, too apt of itself to grow and increase with the possession of power." Locke dismissed the idea that the king is like a father. Paternal power is legitimate because children are not capable of reasoning, but the citizens are capable of reasoning. The king should go by their consent.

Locke was particularly targeting Filmer and not Hobbes because Hobbes was not even defended by the Royalists at that time owing to his atheistic arguments.

Rights of citizens

When Locke said the society cannot give certain rights of the people away to the state, he was referring to rights like freedom of speech, freedom of association and also religious freedom, which is the basis of secularism with which we are familiar in India.

Locke was a Protestant, and the civil war going on in England at that time was partly a conflict between Catholics and Protestants. People were discussing what kind of religion people should have, which religion was better. Locke took the stand that the people should be left free, the state should not take the sides of either the Catholics or the Protestants.

Another important right that Locke stressed was the property right. He was emphatic about people's right to property. How did Locke defend the property right? Man has a right to his body, and so to his labour and to the outcome of the labour that becomes his property. To Locke, the property right is an extension of the right to life.

"The labour of his body and the work of his hands are properly his. Whatever then removes out of the state that nature has provided, and left it in, he has mixed his labour with and joined to it something that is his own, and thereby makes it his property. No man but he can have a right to it, at least where there is enough, and as good left in common for others." Labour is added to something in nature, and that thing becomes the property of the one who added the labour to it.

But this is so only “where there is enough, and as good left in common for others.” This is an important condition. In a situation of water scarcity, a person cannot purify the water and claim it as his own. Locke thus limits the conversion of public resources to private property.

However, Locke doesn’t place any limits on the amount of private property one can acquire. He had no concern about inequalities. This standpoint is supportive of capitalism.

Locke glorified the acquisition of private property. “God gave the world to men in common. It can’t be supposed he meant it should always remain common and uncultivated. He gave it to the use of the industrious and rational; not to the fancy or covetousness of the quarrelsome and contentious.” Those creating private property are “the industrious and rational”. Later, Max Weber would call this attitude towards earning the protestant ethic that contributed to the rise of capitalism.

These are some of the ideas that came to define the modern nation-state. The British and American systems of government and many other modern democracies work on the principles first enunciated by Locke.

The limitations of modern democracies are also the limitations of Locke’s ideas. Rising inequalities is a serious problem in liberal democracies – an issue with which Locke was not concerned.

On the state of nature

Hobbes didn’t think that there was a law of nature, but Locke thought so. Locke’s state of nature is not of war one against other, because there is a law of nature. Locke said, “The state of nature has a law of nature to govern it. Being all equal and independent, no one ought to harm another in his life, health, liberty and possessions.”

Locke makes a distinction between social contract and political contract. The society was formed out of social contract, and a central authority or the state was created out of political contract. A social contract requires unanimity, but a political contract requires only a majority. The government is the trustee of the society, which means sovereignty lies within the society. Locke was an advocate of popular sovereignty. Locke's ideas had a profound impact on political institutions all over the world.

Think on it

1. How is the state formed from the society?
2. What is meant by a negative state?
3. What is the importance of Art. 32 of the Indian Constitution?
4. Why is the separation of powers important?
5. Why are there emergency provisions in the Constitution?
6. Who was Filmer? What are Locke's differences with him?
7. How does Locke defend the property right?
8. According to Locke, can one acquire any amount of property?
9. How are Locke's ideas favourable to capitalism?
10. What does Lock mean by a law of nature?
11. What are Locke's views on the state of nature?

Rousseau

Jean-Jacques Rousseau

CHAPTER THIRTEEN

Obedience as Freedom

Rousseau put forth a concept called "general will". Let's try to understand it. The state is a part of the society, the society impacts the state and the state impacts the society. The state can impact people by educating them and also by punishing them for doing anything wrong.

What kind of relationship is desirable between the state and society? What is an ideal state? What is an ideal society? Rousseau raises these questions. This is where the concept of general will comes in. It deals with a particular relationship between the state and the society and with the nature of the society itself. I want to first convey the spirit behind Rousseau's general will in the context of a family. What is the ideal family that Rousseau imagines, going by the ideal society he has in his mind?

General will in a family

Let us assume that you have your parents, a couple of brothers and sisters in your family. The brothers and the sisters may have their own children too. How in Rousseau's view should your relationship with your family be? Each family member should think about the entire family and not about oneself. Everyone should think about the well-being of the total. One should not think selfishly. This non-selfish thinking on the part of each of its member contributes to a better family.

The family always comes first. Any decision that is taken by anyone in the family should be in keeping with the interests of the whole family. Let's consider a situation where a critical decision needs to be taken. You have fallen in love and you want to marry that person. What does Rousseau expect you to do? Each family member has a say in deciding whether you should marry the one whom you love, and each one should think keeping the whole family in mind.

And if every other member of the family says no to your idea of marriage, then you should go by that decision. Not only should you go by the family decision, but you should also understand that the family is right and you are wrong. You should be thankful to the family because they prevented you from taking a wrong decision.

When you go by the family's decision, you are in fact being free. How is that? To Rousseau, freedom lies in following what is good for all. It would be slavish to follow your desire when that desire can mislead you. The family knows what kind of desires can mislead you. By following the family, you do what is in your own interests, thereby becoming free.

But in case you don't realize that something that goes against your desires can still be in your own interests, then the family could impose its will on you. In forcing you to do something or not do something, they are in fact making you free.

You should therefore understand that your freedom lies in going by the interests of the family, as expressed by all the other family members. It is this freedom you should celebrate, not the freedom of following any petty impulsive desire of yours.

Family decisions turn out to be right, right for all, when everyone thinks for the whole family and not for just oneself. How do we ensure that all the members have this family-first attitude? The family spirit, as opposed to the tendencies of selfish thinking, has to be inculcated in the children through right upbringing.

How should the family ensure that a son or a daughter does not rebel against the family decisions? They should watch the friends of that family member and have any undesirable relations cut off.

Every family member should be isolated from possible evil influences. Such controls are necessary so that the family members learn to go by the family-first ideology and all of them behave in unison like one individual.

When family members become one, a member's interests merge with the family's interests. The ego's interests and the family's interests become one and the same. This is Rousseau's ideal family in which every individual is thinking what he or she is supposed to think as a family member. There is then no conflict between the individual and the family, between self-interest and the spirit of the family. Your will matches with that of the family, your desires match with those of the family.

Because your desires and the family's desires are the same, you are not actually losing your freedom. When you are following the will of your family, you are in effect following your own desire! You should be thankful to have been born in such a family, where you are not losing your freedom as by marrying someone you loved.

So would you want to be a part of such a family? Is that a healthy family? Can it respond to a crisis? Can it adapt itself to social change? Rousseau thought of creating a society like this family. The will of such a society is called the general will. But we should reflect on whether Rousseau's society is actually desirable.

Think on it

1. Give examples of the state and the society.
2. What would be an ideal family to Rousseau, assuming his ideal family is similar to his ideal society?
3. How in your view should an ideal family be?
4. According to you, how should a conflict between the individual will and the family will be resolved?
5. After reading the next lesson, consider whether you would agree that the family described in this lesson mirrors Rousseau's ideal society.

CHAPTER FOURTEEN

The Ideological Road To Totalitarianism

Jean Jacques Rousseau (1712–78) had a great impact on the French Revolution and on the political thought of the world. He was born in Geneva, and he had many unusual ideas partly because he was not formally educated in a university. His books Discourse on Inequality (1754) and Social Contract (1762) conveyed his political ideas. His book Emile (1762) deals with his ideas on education.

Rousseau first became popular through an essay that argued that things that were going on around in his time as a part of Enlightenment did not contribute to real human progress. In this essay written in 1750, he said, “Our souls have become corrupted in proportion as our sciences and our arts have advanced toward perfection.” When everyone was thinking that the world progressed through reason and questioning, Rousseau questioned that view. He felt that compassion was not being developed. The man was only developing reason which was being used for very selfish purposes.

Rousseau had a different kind of ideals in mind than many other thinkers of his time. He had a different political project. He wanted the people to be completely merged with the society as if they became almost one with it. In becoming one with society, man becomes free. Here there is some kind of similarity with Hindu philosophy that says that the individual consciousness becomes free when it merges with the collective consciousness.

General will

Rousseau believed that the state has a very important role in shaping society. The general will is a will for the society. It is not all selfishly worked-out private wills combined, but a will for the society.

Such a will for the society can be generated only under two conditions: (1) When the society is so small that there can be a direct democracy, and not a representative democracy, and (2) When people are relatively equal. Because inequalities would disturb the general will. Particular interests would play out if there are significant inequalities within a society.

Through the right education and appropriate control systems, an environment where people would think for the society should be created. In this ideal society, the individual becomes one with the society in a way that there is no conflict between the individual and the society.

Rousseau's ideal state is relatively egalitarian. Rousseau traces many evils to private property. "The true founder of civil society was the first man who, having enclosed a piece of land, thought of saying, 'This is mine', and came across people simple enough to believe him. How many crimes, wars, murders and how much misery and horror the human race might have been spared if someone had pulled up the stakes or filled in the ditch and cried out to his fellows: 'Beware of listening to this charlatan. You are lost if you forget that the fruits of the earth belong to all and that the earth itself belongs to no one!'"

Rousseau, however, was not for the abolition of private property, he wanted some of it to be there. He was not for absolute equality, but only for relative equality. "Equality must not be understood to mean that power and riches should be equally divided between all, but the power should never be so strong as to be capable of acts of violence. In regard to riches, no citizen should be sufficiently opulent to be able to purchase another, and none so poor as to be forced to sell himself."

A society with extreme inequalities would be full of conflict. "The rich only dreamed only of subjugating and enslaving their neighbours, like those ravenous wolves that, having once tasted human flesh, reject all other nourishment and thenceforth desire only to feed on man."

The modern state was meant to retain the domination of the rich. The rich proposed: "Let us unite to protect the weak from oppression, hold the over desirous in check, and ensure for each the possession of what belongs to him. Let us establish rules of justice and peace." When some had property and others did not have, equal treatment meant perpetuation of inequalities. The government was constituted for the benefit of the rich. "Such was, or must have been, the origin of society and laws ...and henceforth subjected for the benefit of a few ambitious men, the human race to labour, servitude, and misery."

The general will is the will of all the citizens in a direct democracy – which is possible only when the population is small. "Liberty is diminished by the enlargement of the state." When there is an enlargement, direct representation is not possible.

All the people thinking selfishly does not add up to the general will, but everyone thinking of the common good does. "There is often a great deal of difference between the will of all and general will; the latter is concerned only with the common interest, while the former is concerned with private interests, and is the sum of individual wants." The essence of how a good society is to be governed lies in making an individual think in terms of the common good.

Only a relatively egalitarian society can be run by the general will as expressed directly by the people. But small size and egalitarianism would not be enough. For people to be made to think of the welfare of the society over and above their welfare, free opinions should be curbed. Censorship is needed "to preserve morality by preventing the opinions of men from being corrupted."

For people to be made to think non-selfishly for the exercise of the general will, Rousseau wanted a civil religion. In Rousseau's state, there is no freedom of religion. The religion of the state should have certain features. "The existence of a powerful, intelligent, beneficent divinity that foresees and provides; the life to come; the happiness of the just; the punishment of the wicked; the sanctity of the social contract and of the laws."

Christianity is not the right religion for the ideal state. Its otherworldliness is not helpful. "The spirit of Christianity favors tyranny that the tyrant benefits from it. True Christians are made to be slaves; they know it and are hardly bothered by it; since this short life, in their eyes, is worth too little."

Any citizen who does not accept the civil religion may be banished, "for being unsociable and for being incapable of cherishing the laws and justice sincerely, or of sacrificing, when necessary, his life for his duty." The state may execute anyone who "conducts himself as if he did not believe them." Lying before the law is "the greatest of crimes."

Going by the general will is freedom. "Moral liberty is the only liberty that makes man truly the master of himself; for to be driven by our appetites alone is slavery, while to obey a law that we have imposed on ourselves is freedom."

Patriotism, Rousseau says, combines "the force of egoism with all the beauty of virtue." An individual merging with the society for common good is a virtue.

The individual continues to do what he was doing before uniting with society, so he does not lose his freedom. "Where shall we find a form of association which will defend and protect with the whole common force the person and the property of each associate, and by which every person while uniting himself with all shall obey only himself and remain as free as before."

The general will abolishes the distinction between the individual and the collective. Private interests and public interests are merged. "Do you want the general will to be carried out? – ensure that every particular will is in accordance with it; and since virtue is nothing other than this conformity of particular wills to the general, make virtue reign, to put the same thing in one word."

At times when your opinion doesn't match with the general opinion, you should think that the general will is right. "When an opinion contrary to mine prevails, therefore, it proves only that I have been mistaken, and that the general will was not what I had believed it to be. If my particular will had prevailed, I should have done otherwise than I wished; and then I should not have been free."

Supremacy of the state

In Emile, Rousseau writes about how an ideal citizen behaves in his ideal state: "The Spartan Pedaretes presented himself for admission to the council of the Three Hundred and was rejected; he went away rejoicing that there were 300 Spartans better than himself. That was a citizen."

This is equivalent to a hypothetical situation where you write the UPSC exam and the government takes some seven hundred people among whom you are not there and still you feel happy – because there are 700 people better than you. You should be proud of your state because there are 700 people better than you. That is how an ideal citizen thinks.

On the other hand, if you worry that you didn't make it, it would mean that you are being very selfish. If you are living in Rousseau's state and you don't clear the UPSC examination, maybe you should give a party to your friends!

Rousseau gives one more example of an ideal citizen, referring to the Greek state of Sparta. "A Spartan mother had five sons with the army. A helot arrived, trembling she asked the news. 'Your five sons are slain.' 'Was that I asked?' 'We have won the victory.' She hastened to the temple to render thanks to the gods. That was a citizen."

The news that the state won the war was more important to the mother than the death of her five sons. The messenger first told her about her son's deaths, but that was not her immediate interest! This is the kind of thinking that Rousseau advocates.

What happens when a person doesn't think that the general will is right? There is no such option, he should simply think that the general will is right. For example, Rousseau had some strange opinions about women. He wrote in Emile, "Woman is specially made for man's delight." "Little girls always dislike learning to read and write, but they are always ready to learn to sew." Suppose Rousseau's state inculcates such views in the population and even makes them a part of civil religion, then they will be a part of the general will and you will have no scope to disagree.

Even if you are a woman and tend to disagree with such a view, you should think that it is you who is in the wrong. By getting yourself to liking to sew, you are going to be free; by reducing yourself to man's delight, you are going to be free. Because that happens to be what the general will is. You should be thankful to the society for making you like sewing!

J.L. Talmon in his book The Origins of Totalitarian Democracy writes, "Modern totalitarian democracy is a dictatorship resting on popular enthusiasm, and thus completely different from absolute power wielded by a divine-right king, or by a usurping tyrant. Rousseau's general will became the driving force of totalitarian democracy."

Rousseau is regarded as the father of the French Revolution. He was the unofficial ideologue of the French Revolution. The attitudes that he promoted were responsible for a lot of violence at that time. Edmund Burke called him "the insane Socrates of the National Assembly."

Rousseau was given so much respect during the French Revolution that the constituent assembly erected a statue to him in 1790, with the inscription: "The free French nation, to Jean-Jacques Rousseau." In 1794, during the Reign of Terror, a measure was passed to disinter his body and bury it in the Pantheon, where it was placed later that year. Rousseau's influence on Robespierre and other architects of the Reign of Terror is well known. During the French Revolution, even a new religion was also created.

Think on it

1. Why was Rousseau critical of Enlightenment?
2. Why should a society be small for the general will to exist?
3. Why should not there be inequalities for the general will to exist?
4. Was Rousseau for the abolition of private property?
5. Is general will the sum of all private wills?
6. What is the role of civil religion in Rousseau's ideal society?
7. What purpose does censorship play in Rousseau's ideal state?
8. Why was Rousseau against religious freedom?
9. Who is an ideal citizen in Rousseau's ideal state?
10. Did Rousseau influence the French Revolution?

Bentham

Jeremy Bentham

CHAPTER FIFTEEN

Reflections: Are there Natural Rights and Natural Laws?

Man is seen as born with certain natural rights that are considered inalienable. Both Locke and Rousseau proposed that the contract between the individual and the government happens in such a way that an individual's natural rights are not taken away.

The concept of natural rights is also found in the American Declaration of Independence of 1776: "We hold these truths to be self-evident, that all men are created equal, that they are endowed by their Creator with certain unalienable rights, that among these are life, liberty and the pursuit of happiness. To secure these rights, governments are instituted among men, deriving their just powers from the consent of the governed." There is a contract between the government and the people that these natural rights will be preserved.

Similar rights were mentioned during the French Revolution in 1789, in the Declaration of the Rights of Man and of the Citizen. "The goal of any political association is the conservation of the natural and imprescriptible rights of man. These rights are liberty, property, safety and resistance against oppression."

A valid concept?

We need to ask how valid the concept of natural rights is. Take the right to life. We are indeed born expecting to live, but how can we say that there is something like a right to life? Going by Darwin's theory of natural selection, each life form is food for some other life form. As such, one's right to life clashes with another's right to life.

What is a natural right anyway? Does God give it to each child that is born? Does nature assure it? In the natural order of things, each life form is food for some other creature. Humans too hunted many species and drove them to extinction. Didn't they have a right to life too if we have a right to life?

Another right that has been claimed as natural is equality. But there has never been equality among life forms in any species. There is inequality among elephants, giraffes, birds, monkeys and so on. So it is with inequalities among humans. Where does this right to equality come from?

Then there is the right to property, which is also considered natural. But how can it be? You may acquire a certain thing, it is yours, still, you may have to defend it to keep it. If you can't defend it, it could go to others.

When you don't have a natural right over your life itself, you cannot have a natural right over your property. It is all about the survival of the fittest. There is competition for resources everywhere.

Does that mean we shouldn't value these rights? It is not so. We can say there are certain rights that the political system guarantees or should guarantee. We have formed a political association that assures us that we will not be deprived of these basic rights, though they may not be natural and inalienable.

What is meant by an inalienable right? It is a right that cannot be taken away from you. But we find that these rights can be taken away unless protected by some agency.

Elaborate socialist systems are created to bring more equality among people. Much is needed to provide us liberty and safety. So these are not nature-given rights or God-given rights. These are simply ideals of a political system, rights that are promised and protected by it.

Bentham's views

Hobbes, Locke and Rousseau hypothesized a state of nature, but Jeremy Bentham dismisses the idea. He says, "The notion of an actually existing unconnected state of nature is too wild to be seriously admitted." Bentham saw the social contract as some kind of "chimaera", mere "fiction". He did not think there are any natural rights.

Bentham says, "When a man disapproves of a mode of conduct considered independently of any actual system of jurisprudence he says there is a Law of Nature against it. If he can't tell why he disapproves of it he begins talking of a Rule of Right, a Fitness of Things, a Moral Sense or some other imaginary standard which howsoever varied in the description, is from first to last nothing but his own private opinion in disguise."

"Right and legal right are the same thing." Rights not created by the law are a self-contradiction like a "round square" or "cold heat," according to Bentham.

The rights to life, liberty and the pursuit of happiness presented in the Declaration of Independence are "a cloud of words." On the French Declaration of the Rights of Man and of the Citizen, Bentham says: "Natural right is simple nonsense: natural and imprescriptible rights, rhetorical nonsense – nonsense upon stilts."

Edmund Burke too opposed the French Declaration of Rights of Man and of the Citizen and instead made a case that rights spring from within the nation, rather than from nature.

The 20th-century political thinker Hannah Arendt also has a similar view. Arendt says, in The Origins of Totalitarianism: "The Rights of Man had been defined as 'inalienable' because they were supposed to be independent of all governments; but it turned out that the moment human beings lacked their own government had to fall back upon their minimum rights, no authority was left to protect them and no institution was willing to guarantee them. The abstract nakedness of being nothing but the human was their greatest danger." Therefore rights have to be protected by governments and we can't call them natural.

Arendt continues, "It was much wiser to rely on an 'entailed inheritance' of rights which one transmits to one's children like life itself, and to claim one's rights to be the 'rights of an Englishman' rather than inalienable rights of man." Some rights are guaranteed to the citizens because they are the citizens. It's the political system that guarantees rights, not nature.

Bentham, Burke and Arendt are not against rights, but they are against considering some basic rights as natural rights. This is an eminently sensible argument because we tend to call whatever right we think as most basic a natural right, but there is nothing natural about it.

Natural law

To Bentham, the concept of natural law also doesn't make sense. He says natural law is "nothing but a phrase." He says, "Whatever is given for law by the person or persons recognized as possessing the power of making laws, is law." Whatever rule an appropriate authority states becomes the law. Laws are commands issued by the appropriate authorities – this view is called legal positivism.

However, I think that the idea of natural law serves a purpose, unlike the notion of natural right. Just like there are laws related to physical phenomena, such as F = ma, and laws related to the human body, there are also certain laws related to the mind. For example, man has impulses such as sex, aggression, and love. Things like these can be considered a part of natural law. Natural law is nothing but the relationship between many variables we find in nature.

Just like we have medicine, which is about the body, we can have a science about what kind of relationships exists between variables in matters of the mind. This is important because when we make laws, which are called human laws, they should consider natural laws.

Violation of natural laws would have consequences. For example, it is natural for inequality to exist, so if we want to create an equal society, we would have to put in much effort. Understanding such laws of nature is important whatever type of society we want to create, whether we want to be with nature or go against nature.

Living in open subjecting ourselves to rain and sun is what we would do naturally if we didn't have any shelter. But if we construct a house for ourselves, then this is human effort. Still, we can construct a house only following the laws of nature. We can think in the same lines too about the social world. Understanding the nature of man can be the basis for creating the right society. Society can make its laws considering natural laws.

Man needs love, man needs safety, man needs admiration, man is a social being, man prefers privacy too. Such facts about human nature can be considered natural laws. The concept of natural law is needed though the concept of natural rights can be done away with.

Think on it

1. What is meant by a natural right?
2. What are the natural rights mentioned in American Revolution and French Revolution?
3. Why did Bentham oppose the concept of natural rights?
4. What are Arendt's views on natural rights?
5. What are natural laws?
6. What is legal positivism?
7. Should the making of human laws require an understanding of natural laws?

CHAPTER SIXTEEN

Pleasure as Goodness

Jeremy Bentham (1748–1832) did not go with the political theories based on natural rights and social contracts. He wanted to look at things afresh. He said we have to see everything in terms of pleasure and pain; what gives pleasure is good and what gives pain is bad. Pleasure is morally good and pain is morally bad. Pleasure and pain have to be measured in terms of utility, pleasure as something positive and pain as something negative. We can evaluate the basis of any legislation, institution, policy, anything at all, in terms of pleasure and pain. One has to calculate the pluses and minuses associated with a certain thing, and if the plus amounts to more than the minus then we should accept it.

This is the theory of utilitarianism that Bentham proposed. "Nature has placed mankind under the governance of two sovereign masters, pain and pleasure. It is for them alone to point out what we ought to do, as well as to determine what we shall do" (Principles of Morals and Legislation). We have to decide everything with pleasure and pain as our main criteria. "He who adopts the principle of utility esteems virtue to be a good only on account of the pleasures which result from it; he regards vice as an evil only because of the pains which it produces."

Thinking of ethics and morals in terms of pleasure and pain – in terms of the end – is called a teleological approach to morality, 'telos' meaning end in Greek. Bentham would not think of morals in any other way. Thinking in terms of principles and duties rather than the ends of our actions is called a deontological approach, 'deon' meaning necessary in Greek. Bentham proposes a teleological approach to morality, governance and legislation. Everything has to be done with a view of the ends.

To Bentham, there is no difference between one kind of pleasure and another. Any pleasure is the same. The difference between the two pleasures can only be quantitative. This quantity must be measured. If you are proposing legislation, you should calculate its impact in terms of the pleasures and pains it would bring. This is simple arithmetic.

Bentham takes the community as nothing more than "the sum of the interests of the several members who compose it." Community interests are nothing but the interests of the individuals. The individual is given primacy. What should legislation aim at? "It is the greatest happiness of the greatest number that is the measure of right and wrong."

Pleasures are of different types. They can be sex, or power, or something like following a religion, or even something like expressing sympathy. All these pleasures are the same to Bentham. "The quantity of pleasure being equal, push-pin (an early form of bowling) is good as poetry."

How can the quantities of various pleasures be measured? Bentham gives certain variables to help us calculate. For example, *intensity* is one dimension – how intense pleasure or pain is. Then there is the *certainty/uncertainty* dimension. If pleasure is certain, then you add more utilities or units to it, but if it is uncertain, then fewer utilities. If a certain pleasure is worth 50 utilities but has only a 50% possibility of happening, then you can consider it as amounting to 25 utilities. *Propinquity* and*remoteness* are a measure of how soon a pleasure is coming. If it is coming sooner, then it gets more points.

Fecundity is another factor, it means the chance that something will give rise to similar sensations. Sometimes one pleasure leads to many pleasures, in which case it gets more points. *Purity* refers to the likelihood of opposite sensations not arising when one is enjoying something. If pleasure is leading to pain, then the purity of pleasure is reduced. Then there is the factor of the *extent*, meaning how many people are affected. If all these factors are taken into consideration while doing something like making legislation, then it "becomes a matter of arithmetic." This is called 'felicific calculus '.

Even in the case of making criminal law, Bentham wants to go by the calculus. He doesn't think in terms of any religious sanction or other moral principles. He goes only by the principle of maximum happiness to a maximum number of people, which includes the offender whose happiness too should be counted. The pain that the offender receives should be as minimal as possible. The aim of punishment should be only to stop him do it again. It is a purely practical consideration, there is nothing like retribution.

The pain derived from a violation should be more than the pleasure derived from it, considering the probability of not getting caught. Say, a criminal got 1000 plus utilities out of a violation, how much punishment should he get? Only a minimum, which is 1001 minus. But we can't be sure that the punishment will always follow the violation. Suppose there is only 50% certainty this criminal would be caught, then we need to multiply 1001 by 2, which is 2002 minus units. So we give 2002 minus utilities worth of pain to a criminal if the violation he did gave him 1000 plus utilities. This is all mathematical.

"The power of the law need interfere only to prevent them from injuring each other. It is there that restraint is necessary; it is there that the application of punishments is truly useful because the rigour exercised upon an individual becomes in such a case the security of all."

The idea of a negative state or minimal state is implicit in Bentham's theory. "As a general rule, the greatest possible latitude should be left to individuals, in all cases in which they can injure none but themselves, for they are the best judges of their own interests. If they deceive themselves, it is to be supposed that the moment they discover their error they will alter their conduct."

Bentham explains democracy too in terms of utilitarianism. "The greatest happiness of the greatest possible number shall be the object really and constantly aimed at." At that time, Britain had restricted franchise or the right to vote, and Bentham argued for its extension, on the ground that it would lead to the greater happiness of a greater number of people. He also said, "The stricter the dependence of the governors on the governed, the better will the government be." This could be made possible by extending the franchise.

Criticism

There are certain basic problems with Bentham's approach. Consider a hypothetical case of several boys teasing a girl. Suppose the girl experiences the pain of 10 negative utilities and each boy experiences the pleasure of 4 positive utilities. In all there is more pleasure than pain in this activity, so does that mean what the boys are doing is morally good?

During Roman times, the gladiators killed each other while thousands watched them. Again there is much more pleasure than pain in this kind of scenario, so does that make the gladiator contests morally acceptable?

Bentham's approach misses the dimension of rights. To overcome this difficulty, John Stuart Mill argued that all pleasures are not equal. For example, Bentham says: "Call them soldiers, call them monks, call them machines, so long as they are happy ones, I shall not care." Mill however says that there are higher pleasures and lower pleasures. The pleasure that comes out of teasing a girl is lower, the one that comes out of watching some people bleed to death is of a lower kind. In contrast, the pleasure that comes out of helping people and the pleasure that comes out of the pursuit of truth are higher pleasures.

Mill said, "It is better to be a human being dissatisfied than a pig satisfied; better to be Socrates dissatisfied than a fool satisfied. And if the fool, or the pig, are of a different opinion, it is because they only know their own side of the question. The other party to the comparison knows both sides."

Mill extends this logic further to the issue of rights. If a critic expresses his opinions and the others are offended, then their offence is less important. "There is no parity between the feelings of a person for his opinion and the feelings of another who is offended at his holding it, no more than between the desire of a thief to take a purse and the desire of the right owner to keep it."

Does Mill reject utilitarianism on the ground it can't explain rights? No. The rights can be seen as contributing to pleasure in the long run. "Utility in the largest sense, grounded on the permanent interests of man as a progressive being." To Mill, utilitarianism is still valid if we consider the larger picture.

Think on it

1. What is Bentham's theory of utilitarianism?
2. What is a teleological approach as opposed to a deontological approach?
3. How do we decide if legislation is desirable?
4. What is felicific calculus?
5. What variables impact the quantity of pleasure and pain?
6. What is the purpose of punishment?
7. How does Bentham's utilitarianism miss the issue of human rights?
8. Why does J S Mill think that all pleasures are not equal?
9. How can one decide which pleasure is higher?
10. Why should an opinion be expressed even if it is hurtful to others?
11. What is J S Mill's conclusion on utilitarianism?

CHAPTER SEVENTEEN

Reflections: Is Happiness No More than Sustained Pleasure?

Both Bentham and Mill failed to see the difference between pleasure and happiness. This is a very serious limitation of Bentham's theory. The basic idea of utilitarianism is that the amount of pleasure has to be increased and the amount of pain has to be decreased. But the problem with this approach is that in the real world pleasure and pain are closely intertwined.

Think of a simple story where a boy falls in love with a girl, the girl agrees, the parents also approve, and the two of them are happily married. Will that kind of a story make a movie? It won't. In a story, there should be some conflict, some twists, some uncertainty. Something like the parents not agreeing or the girl not agreeing creates conditions for pain. And without the pain, there is no pleasure.

It's the pain of hunger that gives the pleasure of eating. The pain of being insulted makes the pleasure of being recognized possible. The pain of rejection leads to the pleasure of love. The pain of failure brings the pleasure of success. The idea that pain should be minimized and pleasure maximized in all circumstances is misleading as it does not touch upon this link between pleasure and pain.

But if pleasure and pain are so interrelated, what is it that we should seek then? To begin with, we need to make a distinction between happiness and pleasure. These two are clearly different from each other. What kind of thoughts do you have when you are happy? You are likely to think about how you overcame some difficulties, what you achieved, how you did certain things in the right way and so on. Happiness originates more from an internal source, whereas pleasure is derived from an external source.

Happiness is more like a state of mind. When you look in, you are happy. The pleasure on the other hand is a kind of a sensation. Sex is pleasure, but something like the feeling that you behaved rightly in some situation is different, it is happiness. On introspection, you will see that happiness comes out of achievement, overcoming certain difficulties, or the way you handled certain things.

Happiness in a way comes out of how you relate to pain or the meaning you give to pain.

Does this mean we should seek pain? No, that would be self-destructive. But we should not think that we should avoid pain at any cost while seeking pleasure at any cost. Happiness is a matter of us having a healthy relationship with both pleasure and pain – a right kind of relationship with the pleasure-pain cycle. The way you take pleasure and pain determines your happiness.

A happy life does not result from the accumulation of pleasures. It is of a different dimension. You should not try to avoid pain when you have to face it, nor seek pleasure when it is inappropriate to do so. A birthday party or a new year party is an occasion of pleasure, but we should keep in mind that giving parties or going to the parties the year around does not make your life a happy one.

This is about an individual. Now take a country. Consider the long years of India's freedom struggle, during which many people suffered. It had been a time of great pain. But now that pain is a source of pride, a pride that brings happiness. From that pain so many decades ago we got this happiness of our times.

Consider a person acquiring wealth through his efforts; efforts may involve pain, but they become a source of his pride. Similarly, when a group reflects on why it is happy or why it has higher self-esteem, why it is proud of something, it will likely think about the suffering and times of crisis that it went through.

Seeing happiness as a summation of pleasure and aiming at the maximization of pleasure and minimization of pain is conceptually wrong. I'd say this mix-up of happiness and pleasure is a fundamental error of the thinking that underpins modern civilization.

Think on it

1. How are pleasure and pain interrelated?
2. What is the difference between pleasure and happiness?
3. What is the relationship of happiness with pain?
4. What should man seek?
5. What are moments of pride for a nation?

John S Mill

John Stuart Mill

CHAPTER EIGHTEEN

Can Democracy Become a Tyranny of the Majority?

The thought of John Stuart Mill (1806–73) is very relevant to contemporary times. His two major works are Utilitarianism (1861) and On Liberty (1859). In his book On Liberty, he discusses the problems with democracy, rather than those of dictatorship. Before him, thinkers such as Hobbes and Locked talked about monarchy but Mill was more concerned about democracy. He was concerned about how to protect an individual from the oppression of the majority in a democracy.

This question is very relevant now because we live in democratic countries. It is the majority that elects a prime minister or a president, and it is the representatives of these majorities that pass laws. The contemporary problems of unfreedom don't come from a dictator or a tyrannical ruler but from the sway of the majority. So the issue with any democracy is how to protect the rights of an individual from what is called the tyranny of the majority.

Can a good government be chosen through the majority opinion? We don't pick a good scientist from a majority opinion, how can we pick a good leader through a majority opinion? How can the majority find out through the expression of its opinion what is good and efficient government?

Many things have to be judged solely by their merit and not through opinion. Democracy is a rather odd system where you get to determine what is a good government through opinion. Mill tries to find out how such problems, which are very real for contemporary democracies, can be overcome.

Mill says, "The tyranny of the majority is now generally included among the evils against which society requires to be on its guard." He thinks that the rise of the intellectual and moral level of the masses through education is the solution. He called for state-funded education, which was a radical idea then.

However, education can be defective, because there is always the problem of how to educate the educators. The education itself can create the problem of the tyranny of the majority, by pandering to the prejudices of the majority.

Mill considers procedures that can let intellectuals have more say in the government. One way is plural voting, where the members of the intellectual elite get more than one vote each. Mill also proposed a kind of proportional representation where some candidates can get elected with sufficient votes even if they don't get majority votes.

Mill says that the liberty of an individual is good for society. Truth is important for democracy. The truth comes out only when there is freedom of speech. Freedom of speech is not simply a right of an individual, but the need of the political system, particularly in a democracy. Different opinions need to be expressed. "He who knows only his side of the case knows little of that." An opposite view helps. "Truth has to be made by the rough process of a struggle between combatants fighting under hostile banners." There should be a debate to arrive at the truth.

Marcus Aurelius was a wise Roman emperor, but he persecuted the Christians. Mill says, "Unless anyone who approves of punishment for the promulgation of opinions flatters himself that he is a wiser and better man that Marcus Aurelius – let him abstain from that assumption in his devotion of the joint responsibility of himself and the multitude which Aurelius made with so unfortunate a result." You need critical views because you are not infallible.

The majority cannot silence one person, that would be as unjust as one person silencing the majority. "If all mankind minus one were of one opinion, mankind would be no more justified in silencing that one person than he, if had the power, would be justified in silencing mankind."

Diverse types of individualities are needed. "Free scope should be given to varieties of character." Mill believes that people like Socrates are needed for society. "There is always need of persons not only to discover new truths and point out when what were once truths are true no longer, but also to commence new practices and set the example of more enlightened conduct and better taste and sense of human life."

About people like Socrates, Mill says they are "the salt of the earth, without them, human life would become a stagnant pool." Why do we need them so much? Because most people want "to respond to wise and noble things and be led to them."

When will people like Socrates exist? Mill says, "Genius can only breathe freely in an atmosphere of freedom. Persons of genius are more individual than any other people – less capable, consequently, of fitting themselves, without hurtful compression, into any of the small number of moulds which society provides in order to save its members the trouble of forming their own character."

Mill thinks that democracy would be benefited through diverse opinions. Not just freedom of speech, many other freedoms should be given after they are subjected to what Mill called the harm principle. An individual should have as much liberty as possible as long as he is not hurting others. Mill's idea of an ideal state is that of the negative state, just as with Locke.

"The only purpose for which power can be rightfully exercised over any member of a civilized community, against his will, is to prevent harm to others. His own good, either physical or moral, is not sufficient warrant." The state cannot deprive a person of freedom on the ground that it is helping him. Next, "The only part of the conduct of anyone for which he is amenable to society is that which concerns others. In the part which merely concerns himself, his independence is, of right, absolute. Over himself, over his own body and mind, the individual is sovereign."

There can be restrictions imposed on the freedom of speech when it can lead to harm. Opinions can be freely expressed but people are not free to instigate violence. "Opinions lose their immunity when the circumstances in which they are expressed are such as to constitute their expression a positive instigation to some mischievous act. An opinion that corn dealers are starvers of the poor, or that private property is robbery, ought to be unmolested when simply circulated through the press but may justly incur punishment when delivered orally to an excited mob assembled before the house of a corn dealer, or when handed about among the mob in form of a placard."

Mill is clear that the truth has to be expressed, but truth said partially with a motive to cause violence doesn't contribute to wisdom. This position has important implications. Scholarly criticism of a religious scripture is desirable, but reckless talk which is only offensive is not.

Mill is for the education of the masses through the expression of dissent. On the whole, democracy should help improve man. "Human nature is not a machine to be built after a model and set to do exactly the work prescribed for it, but a tree, which requires to grow and develop itself on all sides, according to the tendency of the inward forces which make it a living thing."

A living thing like a tree should be allowed to grow freely, it should not be crippled. "Among the works of man which human life is rightly employed in perfecting and beautifying, the first in importance is surely man himself."

This is closer to Plato's agenda of the improvement of man. The state has to do certain things that will contribute to improving man. One of the things Mill was concerned about is the subjugation of women. He was much ahead of his times in this matter. S. M. Okin, in Women in Western Political Theory, says that "John Stuart Mill is the only major liberal political philosopher to have set out explicitly to apply the principles of liberalism to women."

Mill wrote, "The social subordination of women thus stands out an isolated fact in modern social institutions." "All women are brought up from the earliest years in the belief that their ideal character is the very opposite to that of men; not self-will, and government of self-control, but submission, and yielding to the control of others." "The legal subordination of one sex to the other is wrong in itself and now one of the chief hindrances to human improvement." This kind of subordination should be replaced by "perfect equality, admitting no power or privilege on the one side, nor disability on the other."

Mill was not against the passing of legislation for human improvement or social change. It is not that man is simply to be left as he is and the state need not intervene. How to improve man? How to enhance the level of freedom people have in society? How to protect the individual from the tyranny of the majority? Such were the concerns Mill had and they are very important for contemporary democracies too.

Think on it

1. What is a tyranny of the majority?
2. What role can education play in getting a good government?
3. Why is freedom of speech a need of the system and not simply a right of an individual?
4. Why are people like Socrates needed for democracy?
5. What is a harm principle?
6. What are the limits to freedom of speech?
7. What are Mill's views on women's rights?
8. Is Mill for a minimal state?

Hegel

Fredrich Hegel

CHAPTER NINETEEN

Is there a Spirit?

Friedrich Hegel (1770–1831) is considered a very abstract thinker. Two of his books, Phenomenology of Spirit (1807) and The Philosophy of Right (1821), are very famous. Marx wrote a critique of Hegel's Philosophy of Right as a way of advancing his own theory. Hegel brings the concept of Spirit into his discussion on politics.

What does Hegel mean by Spirit? Here I would like to introduce some concepts with which Indian philosophy is very familiar. Each one of us has a mind, each one of us has consciousness. Consciousness is nothing but a sense of awareness. It is the sense of self. We have a mind and we have consciousness, the sense of me.

This consciousness is not the same thing as the contents of consciousness. By contents, we mean what I am, or my fears, my hopes, my sorrow, my hurt, etc. Consciousness is simply a sense of me, but what I am like constitutes the contents of consciousness. 'I am ' is consciousness, 'I am a good man ', 'I am a bad man' and such are the contents of consciousness.

Indian philosophy propounds that when a man dies, his mind does not die, his consciousness does not die. The mind and consciousness that do not supposedly die constitute the spirit or the soul. A living person is conceived as having a body along with the spirit or soul. Death means the end of the body, but the spirit continues to exist even after death. Consciousness continues, even the mind continues, even if not the complete mind, a part of it. Some memories, feelings, and the 'sense of me' survive death.

This is about an individual. How about humankind? Every individual has a soul, but does humankind as a whole have one?

For humankind

It is written in some Hindu scriptures that humankind has one soul, one spirit. It is called by various names – collective mind, collective consciousness, Soul, Mind, Spirit, world-soul, world-mind. Is there any such thing in reality? Anyway, do individuals have souls?

I wrote on these issues in detail in my book Moksha, Afterlife and Science. My book is based on studies in parapsychology and neuroscience. The conclusions of the book are the following:

- A living person is a combination of body and soul.
- The soul survives the death of a body.
- But there is nothing like a world-soul.

My book disagrees with the philosophy of Advaita which posits that there is a world-soul, the individual soul being only a manifestation of it.

What are Hegel's beliefs? Hegel believes in the world-soul. His term for it is Spirit. Sometimes the same word is translated as Mind, His Phenomenology of Spirit is sometimes translated as Phenomenology of Mind. Hegel does not explain why he thinks there is Spirit. And I have no idea whether Hegel believed in an individual soul.

Hegel discusses the nature of social change at the global level in terms of the changes happening to Spirit. That Spirit refers to that of the whole humankind. Hegel's Spirit which can be very abstract to outsiders could look familiar to the students of Indian philosophy.

Think on it

1. What is the mind?
2. What is consciousness?
3. What is a soul?
4. What is world-soul?
5. What is Spirit?
6. What do you know about Hegel's beliefs?

CHAPTER TWENTY

How Is Spirit Evolving?

In Hegel's words, Spirit is "this absolute substance which is the unity of the different independent self-consciousnesses. 'I' that is 'We' and 'We' that is 'I'" (Phenomenology of Spirit). He equates Spirit with God, "The essence of God – Spirit, the Idea, the world spirit." He says, "The world spirit is the spirit of the world as it reveals itself through the human consciousness; the relationship of men to it is that of single parts to the whole which is their substance" (Reason in History). Spirit is the collective consciousness.

Hegel says that Spirit is changing in two important ways: 1. by growing in freedom, by which Hegel also means increasing rationality 2. by becoming more conscious of its freedom. Not only is it free, but it is also conscious of its freedom. These are the two main trends. Hegel discusses the history of humanity in terms of different stages that manifest increasing freedom as well as increasing consciousness of that freedom.

This history is discussed in terms of the evolution of civilizations. Civilization consists of many states. The different aspects of a civilization are interlinked – art, religion, political system, and so on.

Hegel also explains the dynamics of evolution. Spirit is also called the Idea. Spirit evolves the way ideas evolve in general. How do ideas evolve? Hegel was influenced by Plato's Republic. How does Socrates conduct discussions in The Republic? One participant defines justice as 'giving back what is due.' Socrates asks him, 'If you borrow a knife from someone, will returning the knife to him when he wants to kill someone is justice?' The person agrees that returning in such a context is not justice. Then Socrates asks him, 'What then is justice if returning what is borrowed is not?'

The dialogue follows a pattern: an idea, counter idea, another idea, its counter idea and so on. The first idea is called 'thesis', its opposite is called 'antithesis', thesis and antithesis give rise to synthesis. This synthesis becomes the thesis for the next stage. This process is called dialectics.

In the dialectical process, the truth is arrived at through a resolution of contradictions. Hegel says Spirit also changes in the same way. It evolves through a resolution of contradictions. Civilization develops in a particular way, it reaches a particular stage, and then it cannot grow further, it faces its opposite and then another stage comes.

Hegel identifies four actual civilizations, calling them stages in history. They are 1. the Oriental World 2. Greece 3. Rome 4. and the German world, by which he means Protestant Northern Europe since the Reformation. There has been an increase in the degree of freedom as history moved from one stage to the next stage. "The East knew only that *one* is free; the Greek and Roman world that *some* are free; the German World knows that *all* are free. The first political form in history is despotism, the second democracy and aristocracy and the third monarchy" (Philosophy of History). To Hegel, the highest stage is a monarchy, not democracy. He thought the state he belonged to, the Prussian state, reached a very high stage of evolution.

Hegel calls the first stage, the oriental world – comprising Egypt, India, China, and Persia – the childhood of history. The second stage is adolescence because not all were free due to slavery. The third stage is the manhood of history because positive laws were passed that enhanced freedom and people became more conscious of their freedom. The fourth is full flowering, which is the old age of history. By old age, he doesn't mean loss of strength, but only more maturity.

"World history is the progress of the consciousness of freedom – a progress whose necessity it is our business to comprehend" (Reason in History). He explains, "The Greeks had no conscience; the habit of living for their country without further reflection was the principle dominant among them." Hegel considers, for some reason, the state of people living for their country as an increase in freedom. The Greeks lived so but without being conscious of it. However, in the German world, the Reformation declared "Man is in his very nature destined to be free" (Philosophy of History). The German world was conscious of the increase in freedom.

The vehicle of historical progress is the state. At each stage, an entire civilization is built up around certain states. A civilization's art, religion, and philosophy are connected. Take, for example, how gods evolved. The oriental world had forces of nature as gods, the Greeks had an anthropomorphic conception, and Christianity has the conception of the unity of the divine and human nature. In the first stage, the gods were much away from humans, in the second stage, there was an anthropomorphic conception of the gods. In Christianity, there is unity. People are aware of their growth in Christianity. People's relationship with gods or God has been changing from being very distant to being close.

Some individuals also play a role in this progress, not only states. "The great individuals of world history seize upon this higher universal and make it their own end. It is they who realize the end appropriate to the higher conception of the Spirit" (Reason in History). These important individuals are called 'world historical individuals', e.g., Alexander the Great and Julius Caesar. After Spirit uses them, it discards them. "They fall aside like empty husks." Alexander the Great was important in a particular context, Julius Caesar was important in another context, but after being used by Spirit, they were discarded.

Hegel did not personally see either Alexander or Julius Caesar, but he saw one world historical figure and that was Napoleon. Hegel saw him in Jena after his victory against Prussia. Hegel says in a letter: "The Emperor – this world soul – I saw riding through the city to a review of his troops; It is indeed a wonderful feeling to see such an individual who, here concentrated in a single point, sitting on a horse, reaches out over the world and dominates it."

Why did Hegel think of Napoleon like that? Because Napoleon was seen as contributing to the spread of the ideals of the French Revolution. Hegel would have considered Lenin and Mao also as world souls.

Criticism

But what purpose do these concepts like Spirit, God, and Soul serve? Hegel doesn't explain the sources of these things. Through all these concepts, however, he conveys that history has a pattern. It is the task of a historian to identify the pattern.

Spirit is seen as using certain individuals and states to achieve its end. History is seen as an inexorable process. Marx would retain the idea of history as an inexorable process, dropping the concept of Spirit.

Think on it

1. What is Hegel's definition of Spirit?
2. Mention the two dimensions along which Spirit is evolving.
3. What is the relationship between Spirit and civilizations?
4. What is the Idea, according to Hegel?
5. What is the dialectical method?
6. By what method does Spirit evolve?
7. What are the four stages of history?
8. How is man's relationship with gods changing?
9. Who are world historical figures? How are they related to Spirit?
10. How is history an inexorable process?
11. Can't man influence Spirit?

CHAPTER TWENTY-ONE

Freedom as Obedience to the State

Hegel concludes through a series of certain steps that we should obey the state we belong to. This obedience to the state, he says, is freedom. This is a very strange conclusion. Bertrand Russell comments upon it, saying, "It follows from his metaphysics that true liberty consists in obedience to an arbitrary authority." Russell calls Hegel's philosophy metaphysics, and he is not wrong. The state can be arbitrary, but Hegel concludes that liberty lies in obeying the state. How did Hegel come to this conclusion?

Hegel first says, doing whatever you want to do is not freedom. He has a point here. Freedom is usually defined as the ability to pursue one's desires. But Hegel says that if you follow certain desires, and when those desires don't contribute to your overall well-being, they lead to unfreedom. Addiction is a desire, but it leads to unfreedom. You have many impulses, lustful thoughts, aggressive tendencies and so on, there are so many things in your mind which do not lead to freedom if you pursue them. Hegel is right in saying you can't assume that realizing your desires automatically leads to freedom. Hegel proposes a reflection on the desires – whether a particular desire contributes to freedom or not.

Now he says because your desires need not lead to freedom, do your duty. What is this duty? It is the duty to the state you belong to. Because the state represents an ethical order. How could Hegel say that the state represents an ethical order? Because the state is the means through which Spirit is realizing itself. Spirit is nothing but God. God is realizing his nature through the state, so follow the state and don't go by your desires.

This is a very strange argument. He was right in saying you should reflect on your desires, but how could he say that you should just blindly follow the state, claiming that it leads to your freedom? Surely this doesn't make sense, but that's what Hegel says.

"If we hear it said that the definition of freedom is ability to do what we please, such an idea can only be taken to reveal an utter immaturity of thought" (Philosophy of Right). Yes, this is true.

But Hegel goes on to say, "Impulses, desires and passions and arbitrariness and random inclinations are identified with freedom and that any restrictions imposed upon these are seen as restrictions on freedom itself. On the contrary, such restrictions are the indispensable conditions of liberation" (Reason in History). How can he say any restriction whatsoever is a condition for liberation?

Hegel says about reflection, "An impulse is simply a unidirectional urge and thus has no measuring rod in itself. When reflection is brought to bear on impulses, they are imagined, estimated, compared with one another, with their means of satisfaction and their consequences and with a sum of satisfaction. Reflection purifies it from its crudity and barbarity" (Philosophy of Reason). Yes, we should reflect.

Hegel then talks about duty, "In duty, the individual finds his liberation: first, liberation from dependence on mere natural impulse. In duty the individual acquires his substantive freedom" (Philosophy of Right). "Duty is the attainment of our essence, the winning of positive freedom" (Philosophy of Right). How can every duty be a way to freedom?

Hegel remarks upon marriage as opposed to passion, "Marriage is not to be dissolved because of passion since passion is subordinate to it." He may be right. The difficulty in divorce is to "uphold the right of the ethical order against caprice" (Philosophy of Right). But can we be sure continuing any marriage is ethical and dissolving it would be caprice? It is possible that a particular marriage is not ethical and dissolving it would be ethical!

To whatever state you belong to in whichever part of the world, how can Hegel say that what it does is ethical and when you disobey it, it is caprice? The state itself can be unethical, and you can disobey it as part of following an ethical order. Like Gandhi did, like Socrates did.

To Hegel, any political state is a manifestation of God. "The march of God in the world, that is what the state is" (Philosophy of Right). "The state is the world which Mind has made for itself; its march, therefore, is on lines that are fixed and absolute. Man must therefore venerate the state as a secular deity and observe that if it is difficult to comprehend nature, it is infinitely harder to understand the state" (Philosophy of Right). Here Mind means the same thing as Spirit. If you are seeking divorce, that would mean you have not fully understood marriage, because marriage represents a well-thought-out ethical order.

Whether an individual exists or not doesn't matter much to Hegel. The objective ethical order is permanent. "Mind has actuality, and individuals are accidents of this actuality" (Philosophy of Right). "Whether the individual exists or not is all one to the objective ethical order. It alone is permanent and is the power regulating the life of the individuals" (Philosophy of Right).

The state represents an ethical order and this ethical order is real, the individual is simply an accident. Hegel says so clearly, "The state does not exist for the sake of the citizens; it might rather be said that the state is the end and the citizens are its instruments" (Reason in History). Why is this so? Because Spirit is going in a particular direction and using the state. Spirit is expressing itself through the state, and this state happens to have some individuals.

But there could be different types of states, why can't Hegel think that a particular state itself is an accident? Or Hegel could ask, how can Spirit realize itself through a dialectical process if individuals don't oppose the state?

How does the dialectical process take place? Partly because individuals oppose the state, which they think is not an ethical order. Socrates did not think that the Greek state he lived in represented an ethical order. That is why he rebelled. That is how, one can say Spirit worked through him. Socrates could be Spirit concentrated in a single point, just like Napoleon was. Was Spirit concentrated only in Napoleon?

Hegel's metaphysics doesn't have any objective evidence. It is not logically consistent. Nor is it morally sound. Defining obedience to the state as freedom is in fact immoral. Hegel is wrong on too many counts.

Think on it

1. Should man pursue his impulses without any reflection?
2. What is the role of the state in the march of Spirit?
3. Can every action of a state be regarded as ethical?
4. How is obedience to state equated to freedom by Hegel?
5. Can Spirit work through the dissidents in a state?
6. Can Socrates be taken as Spirit concentrated in a single point?

Marx

Karl Marx

CHAPTER TWENTY-TWO

Is Not the Problem of Alienation Exaggerated?

The concept of alienation is central to Marxism. Karl Marx dealt with it in many of his books such as "Economic and Philosophical Manuscripts" (EP) (1844, published in 1932), "German Ideology" (GI) (1845, published in 1932), "Critique of Hegel's Philosophy of Law" (1844), and "Capital" (Vol.1) (C1) (1867).

Marx believed very clearly that there is something like basic human nature. This, he said, is the characteristic of the species. This basic nature is expressed in a specific way, depending on the mode of production in a particular society. Human behaviour is an outcome of inherent tendencies and economic influences. Marx believed that there is happiness and freedom only when man's basic nature is satisfied, that is when the human essence is satisfied.

Marx says, "Free and conscious activity is the species-character of human beings" (EP). This is also what Hegel said – Spirit moving towards increasing freedom and increasing consciousness of that freedom. Marx speaks highly of consciousness, "What distinguishes the worst architect from the best of bees is this, that the architect raises his structure in imagination before he erects it in reality" (GI). A bee does its work unconsciously, but man consciously.

Criticizing Bentham, a utilitarian philosopher who proposed that man's happiness lies in doing what he likes to do, Marx said, just because a man wants something doesn't mean it is his nature. "To know what is useful for a dog, one must study dog nature. This nature itself is not be deduced from the principle of utility. He that would criticize all human acts by the principle of utility, must first deal with human nature in general, and then with human nature, as modified in each historical epoch" (C1).

Alienation

Marx thought that human essence is expressed and realized through a person's labour. Man's labour should be an expression of himself. Through what he produces, he develops relations with others. In this way he becomes happy. This is also freedom. If a man is not able to express himself through his work and is not related to his product, man would feel he is not being himself. This is alienation. Alienation from the product and his work leads a man to alienation from himself and others.

"The worker, therefore, feels himself at home only during his leisure time, whereas at work he feels homeless" (EP). Feeling homeless at work means the experience of 'This is not me'. This is alienation. "Just as alienated labour transforms free and self-directed activity into a means, so it transforms the species life of man into a means of physical existence" (EP). Work that is supposed to be an expression of our nature becomes simply a means for earning a livelihood. "That man is alienated from his species life means that each man is alienated from others and that each of the others is likewise alienated from human life" (EP).

Ending alienation

Marx wanted to see a society where this alienation would come to an end. He thought technology was causing this alienation, that capitalism and excessive specialization were causing alienation.

The worker is losing control over the process of production. "In handicrafts and manufacture, the workman makes use of a tool;

in the factory, the machine makes use of him" (C1). This is the problem with capitalism: "Within the capitalist system all methods of raising the social productiveness of labour are brought about at the cost of the individual labourer, they mutilate the labourer into a fragment of a man, degrade him to the level of an appendage of a machine, destroy every remnant of charm in his work and turn it into hated toil" (C1).

"The labour exists for the process of production, and not the process of production for the labourer" (C1). Marx's view was: labour for man and not man for labour. "As in religion man is governed by the products of his own brain, so in capitalist production, he is governed by the products of his own hands" (C1). There should not be a religion like this and an economic system like this.

Commodities become important rather than relations. People are after production, without seeing what is happening to the people who are producing the things. This excessive importance given to products is what Marx called commodity fetishism.

Marx wanted a society in which there are fewer goods produced, but in such a way that they don't cause alienation. He says, "The production of too many useful things results in too many useless people" (EP). This is the nature of the modern economy. "The less you are, the less you express your life, the more you have, the greater is your alienated life and the greater is the saving of your alienated being" (EP). To Marx, man should have less to be more. This position is not very different from that of Gandhi.

We wouldn't specialize so much if we gave importance to man rather than to goods. Man has been "a hunter, a fisherman, a shepherd, or a cultural critic and must remain so if he does not want to lose his means of livelihood; while in communist society, where nobody has one exclusive sphere of activity but each can become accomplished in any branch he wishes, society regulates the general production and thus makes it possible for me to do one thing today and another tomorrow, to hunt in the morning, fish in the afternoon, rear cattle in the evening, criticize after dinner, without ever becoming hunter, fisherman, shepherd or critic" (GI).

Is work that important?

If you can work in such a way that it expresses your essence and your unique capabilities, you will be happy. Work satisfaction is indeed an important thing. But isn't Marx exaggerating its importance? Are people so much concerned about what they do?

Most people want to work to get money and success, and through them, they want to win respect, love, and admiration. People are happy that way. This is how they feel related to society. When a person earns a lot of money and constructs a big house, he thinks that he made it out of his work, he feels happy about it. He may feel that it is an affirmation of his competence and himself.

The things that you buy, the things that you give to others, the things you gift, all of them contribute to your relationship with others. The idea that only your work should be your self-expression and otherwise you cannot be related to yourself or others seems hugely exaggerated.

Marx no doubt wrote books as a way of self-expression. Though he did not get any money, he might have been happy. But the idea that others also should be like him, and only then they are humans is a farfetched argument. People work to get money, and through the money, they develop self-esteem and self-respect. They may be lesser beings than Marx, but they wouldn't become alienated beings.

Think on it

1. What is Marx's criticism of utilitarianism?
2. What is the basic species characteristic of human beings?
3. Does the economy affect human motivation?
4. What is alienation?
5. What is commodity fetishism?

6. Is Marx for simple living, just like Gandhi?
7. Why is Marx against specialization?
8. Should a man's work be central to his relationship with himself and others?

CHAPTER TWENTY-THREE

Would Marx Have Approved Leninism?

Would Marx have approved of Lenin's collectivization? Lenin took the land from the peasants and brought it under collective ownership. The agricultural work was supervised by the officials of the communist party, and the workers were paid equal wages. This is what Mao also did later. In both cases, it was done against the wishes of the peasants. What would have Marx said on this?

Erich Fromm says that the main issue that concerned Marx is not the distribution of wealth, but rather alienation. He says: "Marx's central criticism of capitalism is not the injustice in the distribution of wealth; it is the perversion of labour into forced, alienated, meaningless labour." Does this mean that distribution is not an issue? It is an important issue but only as an aspect of the larger problem of alienation.

Some people said that the issue of alienation was important to Marx when he was young but not in the later years. Erich Fromm rejects that view. He says, "The basic ideas on man, as younger Marx expressed them in the Economic and Philosophical Manuscripts, and the ideas of the older Marx as expressed in Capital did not undergo a basic change. Marx did not renounce his earlier views."

In his Economic and Philosophical Manuscripts, Marx made certain explicit statements on what kind of communism he did not want. He says, "Even the equality of incomes which Proudhon demands would only change the relation of the present-day worker to his work into a relation of all men to work. Society would be the conceived as an abstract capitalist." Therefore, through the process of collectivization, you would be turning the society into a capitalist.

Marx did not want to replace individual capitalists with the community. "The community is only a community of work and equality of wages paid out by the communal capital, by the community as universal capitalist."

He clearly says, "The role of the worker is not abolished but is extended to all men." Instead of having landlords and the workers, all are made into workers. This is not what Marx wanted.

Marx is against the idea of 'you can't have what others can't have '. He rejects that brand of communism – which he calls crude communism. He says, "In crude communism, the domination of material property looms so large that it aims to destroy everything which is incapable of being possessed by everyone. It wishes to eliminate talent by force. Immediate physical possession seems to it the unique goal of life and existence."

We can't say that Marx was against any kind of private ownership. "The tendency to oppose general private property is expressed in animal form; marriage (which is a form of exclusive private property) is contrasted with the 'community of women,' in which women become common property. One may say that this idea of the community of women is the open secret of this entirely crude and unreflective communism." Making things common to all can be as bad as turning wives into prostitutes! "Just as women are to pass from marriage to universal prostitution, so the whole world of wealth is to pass to the relation of universal prostitution with the community."

The basis of communism can't be envy. Marx says, "Crude communism is only the culmination of envy and levelling-down on the basis of a preconceived minimum."

Marx's statements on crude communism can be taken as evidence that he would have opposed Lenin's collectivization, which made the peasants work like serfs on their own lands under the party supervision.

Think on it

1. What is meant by making a society a capitalist?
2. How can making property public be equated to prostitution?
3. What is crude communism?
4. Should all property be only in private hands?
5. Is alienation an important factor in deciding what should be made public?

CHAPTER TWENTY-FOUR

To Have a Society Without a State

Marx's dream of a society without alienation would not be easy to realize. It would be, in a way, a spiritually evolved society – because in that kind of society there would be no conflict between essence and existence, there would be no conflict between becoming and being. To Marx, socialism is a society's highest attainment: "It is the true solution of the conflict between existence and essence, between freedom and necessity, between individual and species. It is a solution of the riddle of history and knows itself to be this solution" (EP).

Erich Fromm says that Marx was deeply religious and his atheism was an advanced form of "rational mysticism, closer to Meister Eckhart or Zen Buddhism." Fromm says: "Marx wrote as a motto for dissertation, 'Not those are godless who have contempt for the gods of the masses but those who attribute the opinions of the masses to the gods.'" To Marx, if you think you will get your wishes fulfilled by praying, you are being godless!

Fromm writes, "Socialism (in its Marxist and other forms) returned to the idea of the 'good society' as the condition for the realization of man's spiritual needs." "It was antiauthoritarian, both as far as the Church and the State are concerned, hence it aimed at the eventual disappearance of the state and at the establishment of a society composed of voluntarily cooperating individuals."

The goals of Marxism are far higher than the much simpler goals of liberalism. Fromm says: "Liberalism had to insist not only on separation from State and Church but had also to deny that it was the function of the state to help realize certain spiritual and moral values; these values were supposed to be entirely a matter for the individual."

Materialism

Marx believed that socialism would come. It would come about not through ideas, education, and religion, but economic changes. Hegel's theory is called idealism, which meant ideas change society, but to Marx, the changes in ideas are a result of changes in the economy. The economy changes first and then other things in society change, including consciousness.

To Marx, economy and technology constitute "the base" of the society on which the other aspects of society – politics, education, the religion that constitute "the superstructure" – depend. The techno-economic base influences the superstructure. This theory is called materialism, as opposed to Hegel's idealism.

The source of social change to Marx is not politics and the state, as they are only a part of the superstructure which is impacted by the base that is the economy.

Marx rejects Hegel's concept of Spirit. "Hegel's philosophy of history presupposes an abstract or absolute Spirit, which develops in such a way that mankind is only a mass which carries this spirit, consciously or unconsciously. Hegel assumes that a speculative, esoteric history precedes and underlies empirical history. The history of mankind is transformed into the history of the abstract spirit of mankind, which transcends the real man" (The Holy Family, 1845).

"The general result at which I arrived and which served as a guiding thread for my studies can be briefly stated as follows: in the social production of their life, men enter into definite relations that are indispensable and independent of their will, relations of production which correspond to a definite stage of development of their material productive forces." Material productive forces mean technology, it is a technology that leads to a particular kind of relations of production. Technology, as well as relations of production, are a part of the base.

"The total of these relations of production constitutes the economic structure of society, the real foundation, on which arises a legal and political superstructure and to which correspond definite forms of social consciousness. The mode of production of material life conditions the social, political and intellectual life process in general." This base, also called the mode of production, conditions all the other aspects of society.

"It is not the consciousness of men that determines their social being, but, on the contrary, their social being that determines their consciousness" (Contribution to Critique of Political Economy). Man's social being determines his consciousness, his social being in turn is determined by his economic position.

"At a certain stage in their development, the material productive forces of society come in conflict with the existing relations of production, or with the property relations within which they have been at work hitherto. From forms of development of the productive forces, these relations turn into their fetters. Then begins an epoch of social revolution. With the change of the economic foundations, the entire immense superstructure is more or less rapidly transformed." Technology changes first, then the relations of production change. With these changes, everything else changes.

The world had gone through such changes several times in the past. "In broad outlines, Asiatic, ancient, feudal and modern bourgeois modes of production can be designated as progressive epochs in the economic formation of society." India's caste system reflected an Asiatic form of production. The Greek city-states were part of an ancient mode of production. Then came feudalism. The 'modern bourgeois mode of production' simply means capitalism. Marx sees these changes as being progressive – keeping with

Hegel's idea of historical progress.

Marx says the present mode of production is not the last one, it is going to be replaced by communism. He predicted that capitalism would lead to huge inequalities, there would be relatively few capitalists and a huge proletariat with very low wages. The proletariat would eventually revolt and establish what is called the dictatorship of the proletariat, which is an intermediary stage before they go for a communist society. Marx thought that all this would happen due to inherent contradictions in capitalism. All of this is inevitable in the process of history.

Then human nature will change too. "What they are coincides with their production, both with what they produce and with how they produce. The nature of individuals thus depends on the material conditions determining their production" (GI).

No state

The relations of production in society are reflected in the relations between the classes. In ancient society, the classes were masters and slaves; in a feudal society, landlords and serfs; and in a capitalist society, capitalists and the proletariat. In a communist society, there would be no classes.

The communist society, according to Marx, does not need a state. Because the state exists only to serve the dominant classes. Political power as such would not exist in a communist society. "Political power, properly so called, is merely the organized power of one class for oppressing another" (The Communist Manifesto).

Marx thought of the state as an instrument of violence or a source of an ideology that enables class domination. "The executive of the modern state is but a committee for managing the common affairs of the whole bourgeoisie" (Works I). Addressing the people of the bourgeois class, Marx said, "Your jurisprudence is but the will of your class made into a law for all, a will, whose essential character and direction are determined by the economic conditions of existence of your class" (Works I).

The state comes from the civil society, but under communism, the civil society will be changed in such a way that the state would not be needed anymore. "Since the state is the form in which the individuals of a ruling class assert their common interests, and in which the whole civil society of an epoch is epitomized, it follows that in the formation of all communal institutions the state acts as an intermediary, that these institutions receive a political form" (GI).

When civil society changes in the direction of communism, the state will cease to exist. "The working class in the course of its development will substitute for the old civil society an association which will exclude classes and their antagonism, and there will be no more political power properly so called since political power is precisely the official expression of antagonism in civil society" (Poverty of Philosophy). The old civil society was the one with classes, but the new one would not have any classes in it.

Engels writes in his book Socialism: Utopian and Scientific, "As soon as there is no longer any social class to be held in subjection, nothing more remains to be repressed, and a special repressive force, a state, is no longer necessary. The government of persons is replaced by the administration of things, and by the conduct of processes of production. The state is not 'abolished '. It dies out." The state dies out, this is also called the withering away of the state.

Engels says that "the government of persons is replaced by the administration of things". Some structure may exist for simple coordination, but Marx and Engels wouldn't call it a state – for it is not going do any kind of propaganda or repress any class of people.

Think on it

1. Why does Erich Fromm say Marx's atheism is similar to Buddhist atheism?
2. What is a socialist society, according to Marx?
3. What is Hegel's idealism?

4. What is Marx's materialism?
5. What constitutes the base and superstructure of a society?
6. What, according to Marx, is the way to change human consciousness?
7. What is the mode of production in a society?
8. What is meant by relations of production?
9. What are the stages of world history according to Marx?
10. How will capitalism lead to communism?
11. What is the difference between civil society and the state?
12. What is the role of the state in a society with classes?
13. What happens to the state under communism?

Bernstein

Eduard Bernstein

CHAPTER TWENTY-FIVE

Evidence by 1900 that Marx Was Wrong

Eduard Bernstein (1850–1932) is a very important thinker, who was first a Marxist, and later converted to what is called democratic socialism. He was one of the earliest thinkers who found out what was wrong with Marxism, empirically as well as theoretically. Bernstein was very close to Engels. He knew how certain theoretical positions were derived in Marxism. He also understood that the communism developing around that time was not a desirable development.

Bernstein was born in Berlin, in a Jewish family. He joined the Social Democratic Party in 1872. The anti-socialist laws of Bismarck drove him in 1878 to exile in Switzerland, from where he went to London. He was impressed by the political economy of Britain, and he came under the influence of the Fabians.

He believed what the communists of that time were planning was wrong. He was instrumental in driving German social democracy away from the Bolshevik fantasies after the end of WW I. He condemned the attempted seizure of power by the communists in Germany. He died 6 weeks before Hitler came to power. He had made powerful speeches against Hitler but never thought that Nazism would become as powerful as it became.

Marx and Engels wrote the Communist Manifesto in 1848; Marx died in 1883, and Engels in 1895. By the end of the nineteenth century, capitalism was changing. It had been changing even during

Marx's time, but Marx and Engels did not update their Manifesto and they did not change their thinking. Bernstein studied what was going on in the economy and felt the need to revise the Marxist doctrine.

Bernstein thought he was doing a kind of revision of Marxism. It was called revisionism within Marxism. Revisionism was originally a school of thought with Marxism, but later it gathered negative connotations when the Bolsheviks started calling their enemies revisionists. Bernstein however continued to call himself a revisionist.

Capitalism working differently

What did Bernstein find? Marx predicted that in the advanced stage of capitalism, there would only be a few capitalists remaining along with a huge number of the proletariat. This polarization was what Marx expected. But by the end of the nineteenth century, Bernstein found that this polarization was not happening. He wrote his observations in Evolutionary Socialism: A criticism and Affirmation (1899). There were more capitalists around at that time than earlier, and there also were multiple classes. This was not the way Marx thought capitalism would work.

Marx thought that the proletariat would be progressively more miserable. But Bernstein found this was not true. The wages were going up. Bernstein found that everybody was getting better off in capitalism. The kind of polarization that was expected to be the ground for a revolution was not happening. Marx's Das Kapital was thus found to be empirically wrong. What were the implications of this?

It meant Marxism is not a science, the proletarian revolution was not inevitable. Lenin and others were saying that the revolution was inevitable and they were only fast-forwarding it. Bernstein did not think so. To him, the proposals of Marx were only ethical principles, ideas on how people should live, they were not scientific principles.

Revising the theory

Bernstein examined the Marxist theory, based on what he observed about the ways of capitalism. The central theory of Marxian economics is about determining the value of a product. Marx felt that this value comes from human labour. Remember that these theories were being worked out before it became known that price is a result of demand and supply forces, which Alfred Marshall found out much later. Before Marshall, the economists were trying to work out why people pay more for some things and less for other things, and there were many theories. Marx propounded that the value is coming from human labour. The difference between price and wage is surplus. Marx called this surplus exploitation.

In an unusual way of thinking, Marx was considering only human labour. Bernstein questioned this approach. He found that in the industries where there were more profits, there were higher wages. Marx thought that when the capitalists competed for higher profits, they would lower the wages. Bernstein found that the higher profits were not due to lower wages and that these higher profits were leading to higher wages.

If the wages are higher and profits are high too, Bernstein thought, what is this theory of value? He understood that what constitutes value is not only the labour of hands or the proletarian labour, as Marx thought, but there is also the mental labour of many other people, be it managers, be it bankers. Many people are contributing to the value addition, so Marx's idea that only the labourers are contributing to value, and everybody else is an exploiter is wrong. The banker is contributing, the engineer is contributing, the capitalist is contributing, so many people are contributing to a product's value.

If a good is selling at a higher price, people in various occupations have contributed to that price, so all these people deserve a share in the profit. Bernstein found that there are more specialists in capitalism, more classes and more contributions from diverse sources. If others are also contributing to the value of a product, besides the workers, then what does it mean? It amounts to a serious criticism of Marxian economics.

More seriously, Bernstein thought that when many people with different specializations are doing things and finally getting benefited out of improving a product, why should we think of conflict between classes? The same thing can be thought of in terms of cooperation, rather than conflict.

Capitalism was improving, people were cooperating, everybody was better off. There were negotiations between the capitalists and the workers, the workers were demanding certain things and the capitalists were improving the working conditions. Cooperation and dialogue between classes were possible.

Marx thought that the capitalists would use the state in their exploitation; Bernstein said that if capitalism was changing and cooperation was possible, the state also could change. Gradually, cooperatively, all the stakeholders could change the nature of the state.

Communism difficult

When there are more capitalists and more classes, evolving systems of collective ownership also becomes more difficult. Going for collective ownership would not be possible when the ownership is not within just a few hands. In Germany of Bernstein's time, there were around one million small and big enterprises in all. Bernstein wondered how all of them could be nationalized. He proposed democratic socialism: go for democracy and evolve better patterns of ownership, working towards creating a more just society.

Giving more power to the workers' councils is democracy. The parliament, local self-government and workers councils are all part of a democracy. Bernstein was thinking in terms of the economic empowerment of people of various groups using democracy, through dialogue and cooperation. He was thinking in terms of giving property to people to empower them, not taking away their property to realize a particular ideal.

Bernstein knew that as long as there are classes, there would be inequalities. Democracy is not perfect, there would be class differences even in a democratic society. But this should change.

In the end, democracy should bring a government that is not pandering to any particular class. To Bernstein, democracy is an 'absence of class government'. He wanted to use democracy to change the nature of the state and to use the state to change the nature of the economy and democracy.

Evaluation

How do we evaluate Bernstein's critique of Marxist economics? Bernstein was far ahead of his time, he understood the limitations of Marxism. Had Lenin followed Bernstein's suggestions, the history of the world would have been very different.

Was Bernstein right in thinking that democratic socialism would one day lead to a government that is not class-biased? It doesn't seem so. Bernstein's democratic socialism did not create any such government or any kind of new society. But it was good enough to identify the problem with Marxism. If only Bernstein's advice was heeded, a lot of unnecessary violence would not have taken place.

Think on it

1. What is meant by revisionism in the context of Marxism?
2. What predictions of Marx turned out to be false by the end of the 19thcentury?
3. What is wrong with Marx's theory of value?
4. Why should mental labour too be considered in determining the value of a product?
5. In what sense was capitalism benefiting all?
6. Why is Marx's idea of class conflict not entirely true?

7. Why would communism be more difficult to achieve when there are more classes?
8. What in the end is the goal of democracy?

Lenin

Vladimir Lenin

CHAPTER TWENTY-SIX

Leninism: A Huge Wrong Turn in History

Vladimir Lenin (1870–1924) played an extremely important role in shaping the concept of a communist state. In doing so, he influenced twentieth-century world history in a major way. Lenin tried to apply Marxism in his country Russia. He was interested in overthrowing the Russian government even before he read about Marxism. His brother was executed in 1887 for his participation in a plot to kill the Czar. Lenin's family was condemned by the state for that act. Lenin's brother was such a person that though he was allowed to seek forgiveness, he preferred to be hanged. Lenin was inspired by his brother and got interested in the overthrow of the czarist regime.

Lenin started studying Marxism in 1883 and then became a member of the Russian social democratic party. It was this party that later split into Bolsheviks and Mensheviks. Lenin's faction was called Bolsheviks, and after the Revolution, Lenin called it the Communist Party. Lenin wrote books such as Imperialism: The Highest Stage of Capitalism (1917) and The State and Revolution (1917). He first laid out his agenda in 1902 in "What is to Be Done?" He also shared his thoughts in a newsletter, Iskra, which meant the spark.

Lenin was trying to apply Marxism to the Russian conditions. Marx wrote that advanced capitalism would create conditions for revolution, and such conditions would arise in France or the UK or possibly even in Germany. But Marx did not think of Russia, as it was primarily an agrarian economy and industry was not developed much. This proletarian revolution was supposed to be an inevitable process, emerging out of the laws of history. Marxism was supposed to be a science.

However, in The Communist Manifesto (1848), Marx and Engels called for action even under conditions not ripe for a proletarian revolution. About Germany, they said that the bourgeois revolution there would only be the prelude to a proletarian revolution. Lenin understood that Marx was referring to the possibility of such a revolution in Germany of 1848. He thought that the Russia of his times was closer to the Germany of 1848.

Lenin made it explicit that conscious action by the intelligentsia is needed to expedite the proletarian revolution, even when capitalism is not at an advanced stage in society. He wrote: “The theory of socialism grew out of the philosophic, historical and economic theories that were developed by the educated representatives of the propertied classes, the intellectuals. The founders of modern scientific socialism, Marx and Engels, were themselves, in social position, members of the bourgeois intelligentsia. Similarly, in Russia, the theoretical doctrine of Social Democracy arose entirely independently of the spontaneous labour movement. It arose as a natural and inevitable outcome of the development of the thought of the revolutionary intelligentsia” (What is to Be Done?).

The entire movement of socialism was a result of Marxist ideas, not of labor movements. “Spontaneous development of labour movement leads precisely to its subordination to bourgeois ideology. The spontaneous labour movement is trade-unionism. Trade-unionism means the ideological enslavement of the workers by the bourgeoisie” (ibid).

Lenin concluded that a group of people have to bring about the revolution to facilitate communism. The communist party was supposed to serve this function. How was the party different from the proletariat? To Lenin, the party represented an ideological leadership, it was for the proletariat but it need not be composed of the proletariat only. What was the problem if the party was composed only of the proletariat?

In the conditions of Russia of that time, the proletarian class was too small and not enough to make a revolution happen. One could not depend only on the proletariat. There was the peasantry too. In Marx's scheme, there was little role for the peasantry. Marxism meant a movement towards communism, the absence of private property. The proletariat would welcome it, but why would the peasants want it? The peasants would agree to land redistribution from rich farmers to the poor ones, but why would they be willing to surrender their own land?

Lenin thought that as long as the peasants were demanding land redistribution they would be on the side of the revolution, but when they start opposing handing their land over to the communes, they would become counter-revolutionary. Lenin's concerns were thus a too small proletariat and a counter-revolutionary peasantry. The party should handle the issues related to the peasantry, and the party should also increase the size of the proletariat in the future, which would require industrialization.

Lenin and other revolutionaries were working on these issues because they knew some major political event would happen in the Russian state, though they did not predict the 1905 revolution or the 1917 revolution. The Russian state was weakened by external wars. In 1905, it was the war with Japan, and in 1917, it was the war with Germany. These two wars gave rise to two revolutions in Russia. But the 1905 revolution was a small one, more like a rehearsal to 1917. Both of them were not expected, but those influenced by Marx were thinking something was going to happen.

Imperialism

Lenin also worked on imperialism. To Lenin, imperialism was a higher stage of capitalism. Why would a country want to dominate another country? To obtain raw materials or to get a market for finished products. Lenin thought that this desire for domination would lead to wars. He believed that imperialism would spread capitalism to many countries, and when capitalism spreads, the possibility of proletarian revolutions also spreads.

Lenin thought that the proletariat in Russia would be assisted by the proletariat in other countries. The revolution in Russia would be sustained through the revolutions in other countries -- this was the theory of a permanent revolution. It was championed by Trotsky. Proletarianism in Russia would be supported by other countries and then a communist leadership would guide these countries – this was the vision of Leninism. Lenin had that international outlook, he thought in terms of classes and economic ideologies, rather than nations.

That was why Lenin thought a party was needed. But the problem with a party was that it would consist of not only the proletariat but many people with revolutionary ideology, whichever class they may be representing.

The Russian revolutionaries were thinking not only about The Communist Manifesto but also about the French Revolution and the Paris commune. The French Revolution happened in 1789, the Paris commune happened in 1871. In the Paris commune, workers' councils were formed and they attempted to build an independent community, but those efforts ended in a disaster. During the French Revolution, enormous violence took place. It was said that much violence took place because the party of Jacobians did not have a base in any class. The Marxists were concerned about how to avoid such failures in the future.

Trotsky was not with Lenin when the party split, he was with the Mensheviks. Trotsky criticized Lenin on the ground that the party did not represent the proletariat, and that it was being used as a substitute for the proletariat. He said that the central committee could become a substitute for the party in the future, and this central committee would have one leader. This was a road to dictatorship. It happened eventually, in the absence of independent institutions such as legislature and judiciary to check the power of the executive as in liberal democracies.

A centralized structure was created by Lenin himself. What Lenin created, Stalin expanded and made far worse. Later, Mao followed a similar thing in China. Russia imposed its brand of communism on its allies later. The Marxian theory was given a particular kind of application by Lenin and became communism. It was Lenin's application of Marxism that finally created what we know as the communist state. Probably if Lenin was not there, then Marx would have remained simply a critic of capitalism and ideological inspiration for people to create a less unequal society.

Workers in an industrial setup may want to be part-owners, but why would farmers want to give away their land? It is wrong to think that people would not want private ownership of the resources. It is reasonable to think that the workers' councils would want to end private property because that would be ending the private property of their owners. In the case of peasants, however, once the landless get the land why would they want to give away their lands to the government?

The idea that people would want communism is wrong. Such communism can only be imposed violently from the above. That's what Lenin started and Stalin continued. The creation of a large proletariat in the Soviet Union required massive industrialization, a process that led to a great deal of violence.

Think on it

1. What economic system according to Marx would give rise to a proletarian revolution?
2. Why was Russia an unlikely country for a proletarian revolution?
3. Can a non-proletarian revolution do good for a country according to Marx?
4. What is the role of the intelligentsia in a proletarian revolution?

5. What was the role of the communist party in the Russian Revolution?
6. Why would the peasantry be counter-revolutionary?
7. What is the theory of permanent revolution?
8. Why would socialism in one country need socialism in other countries?
9. Would people want the abolition of private property?

CHAPTER TWENTY-SEVEN

Was Lenin Squeezing Russia to Fit Das Kapital?

When we think of the Russian Revolution of 1917 that brought communism, we tend to assume that people brought it about voluntarily fighting against the autocratic government of the Czar. It was portrayed as a case of people against the autocratic government. But on closer examination, it doesn't seem to be so.

To begin with, the Russian government was weakened because of the 1905 war and World War I. The Czars were already brought down and a provisional government was ruling Russia when the Bolsheviks overthrew it in a coup. Lenin came to power overthrowing the provisional government of that time. The civil war followed later. In the end, Lenin consolidated his power.

Did Lenin communicate his idea of communism to the people or to the groups whose support he was seeking? No. Different groups supported Lenin for different reasons. Lenin promised to implement a popular demand that Russia be brought out of the war. Lenin promised power to the workers' councils. He promised land reforms for which there was support from the peasants. But he did not advocate communal ownership of land, for which there would be no support. He created a powerful party, a powerful secret police – all without any popular support.

Marx thought that in advanced capitalism, there would be a huge proletariat and in the end they would rebel. Whatever was predicted in Das Kapital, Lenin wanted to fast forward it. Towards that end, he wanted to create a larger proletariat in Russia. So there had to be more industrialization. Lenin did not think about the peasants, "Okay, if there is a large agricultural population, what should communism mean to them?"

Lenin promised land reforms, people thought those who did not have enough land would get land and they supported it. Lenin believed that this kind of transfer of property from the rich to the poor is a part of the revolution. He knew that once the peasants got the land, they would not give it back, they would become counter-revolutionary. He thought the peasants were backward-looking and they wouldn't understand communism. These peasants had to be forcibly made property-less, then communes could be developed.

Marx did not see any revolution coming from the peasants. Lenin too did not see such a thing. The peasants should be forcibly dispossessed, and they should live in communes. This would be a party-led effort. First a class war was provoked so that the poor would fight against the rich. Once the rich were eliminated, everybody who opposed handing over the land would be eliminated.

In effect, what was Lenin doing? He was trying to squeeze the Russian society to fit a book, Karl Marx's Das Kapital – fast-forwarding the process predicted by Marx. That was why he had to inflict a lot of violence, and people were not a part of this kind of communism.

Lenin knew that there was not a large enough proletariat, and so he thought that there should be support from the proletariat classes of other countries to the communist revolution. The revolution should not be confined to Russia, it should spread to other countries also. Lenin was trying to create a society that was suitable for communism in Russia.

In theory, there was little scope for action in Marx's Das Kapital, as things were supposed to happen inevitably through the inherent logic of capitalism. But Lenin was trying to use reason, coercion, and the party to create such conditions, to bring about the revolution. And there was no participation by the people in all this. It was just one man's idea.

Under the banner of communism, Lenin took the produce of the farmers overcoming so much of their resistance. In May 1918 Lenin declared that the owners of surplus grain who refused to turn it in, regardless of their social status, rich or poor, "will be declared enemies of the people."

When the Russian economy was crumbling in March 1921, Lenin announced a new economic policy through which capitalism was introduced. This policy was meant to be in implementation only for a brief period till the economy becomes strong enough for socialism.

Between 1929 and 1933, during Stalin's era, 10 million people died as a result of the collectivization drive in agriculture, mostly due to famines. Many people became beggars. Stalin created farms that would be party-run. Stalin's leadership was ideologically justified on the ground that if he did not do it by force, why would the peasants cooperate with the government? How can anybody agree to collectivization, how can anybody voluntarily give away their property?

Stalin thought, and many agreed, that only he had that determination and will to implement Marxism and Leninism. That was Stalin's source of legitimacy.

The same authoritarianism was seen during the phase of industrialization also. Many people lost their land and they were brought to the industry. Many others were jailed. It is estimated that in the 1930s, 10% of Russian GNP was produced by prisoners. There was coercion in the process of industrialization and there was coercion in agriculture. This coercion was justified on the ground that they were going to create a communist society, "If we don't do this, how can communism come?"

This is the real nature of the Russian Revolution. Neither Lenin nor Stalin asked the basic question about the validity of Marxism, maybe Marx was wrong, maybe people don't want communism, maybe a better society need not be envisioned in terms of the absence of private property. Or if Russia does not have advanced capitalism, how should communism be defined for the Russian society? Lenin did not ask such questions which we can think of as legitimate questions. Much of the violence was perpetrated by these leaders in trying to squeeze the Russian society to fit the conditions that Marx wrote about.

Think on it

1. What role did Lenin play in the 1917 revolution?
2. In what sense was1917 a year of revolution for Russia?
3. What were the promises that Lenin made during the Russian revolution?
4. Why did Lenin want to go for industrialization?
5. What was the policy of Lenin towards agriculture?
6. Why did farmers oppose collectivization?
7. What was the context of the New Economic Policy?
8. Was there continuity between Lenin's policies and Stalin's policies?
9. Why did the communist state become violent?

Gramsci

Antonio Gramsci

CHAPTER TWENTY-EIGHT

Is Not Counter-hegemony as Bad as Hegemony?

Antonio Gramsci (1891–1937) was an Italian Marxist thinker, who is known for making some innovations to Marxism. He joined the Italian Socialist Party in 1913. In 1919, he founded a weekly called New Order, which focused on applying the lessons of the Russian revolution to the Italian conditions. He influenced the workers' movements that led to strikes and factory occupations in 1920. Because of the unrest with which he and the entire movement of socialism were associated, the landed aristocracy and factory owners supported the rising fascist movement of Mussolini. Gramsci founded the Italian Communist Party in 1921. Because of his political activities, he was jailed in 1926. He was released only when his death was imminent due to failing health. He wrote 34 notebooks when he was in jail, which were smuggled out. Those notebooks became popular and people got to know many of his ideas.

Gramsci was exploring why the communist revolution was not taking place in Italy as it was supposed to take place if Marx was right. It would seem like there were many things that Gramsci accepted from Marx without a critical examination of Marx.

Marx believed that advanced capitalism would result in there being a few capitalists and a large number of the proletariat. Marx said that it was from the proletariat that the revolution would come. Gramsci was asking why the workers in Italy were not going on strikes and planning a revolution. However, there really was no reason to think that the conditions that Marx predicted were attained in the Italy of Gramsci's time.

The proletarian revolution took place by 1917 in Russia, and Gramsci was asking how it could happen in Russia and not in Italy. What were the conditions in Russia? Gramsci did not see the Russian revolution as an outcome of some accidental factors. There had been political instability which Lenin used to make a revolution happen. Gramsci's question of why it happened in Russia and not in Italy was not a very valid one. Moreover, by accepting the 1917 revolution as a communist revolution, Gramsci was also endorsing Lenin's kind of communism.

Gramsci was questioning why a revolution was not taking place in Italy. According to him, the Italians had to go for a revolution. But it is not clear why it had to be so. The conditions as predicted by Marx were not there. The peculiar situation that Russia had been in was not there in Italy. But these facts did not stop Gramsci from asking why a revolution was not happening. It did not stop Gramsci from attempting to answer his essentially wrong question. However, in this process, he made some important contributions to the way Marxism worked.

Towards idealism

To Marx, the economy and technology are the base of society, and all others are the superstructure. The bourgeois classes control what the entire society thinks, through the institutions of religion, education, media, which are a part of the superstructure. The ruling classes create structures, which make the entire society think in a particular way. They make society think in a way that is convenient to them. Social consciousness is thus impacted by the interests of the ruling classes.

Gramsci thought that the workers in the Italian society were not thinking in terms of a revolution because they were being manipulated by the ruling classes. The bourgeois classes flooded the collective consciousness in a particular way. Gramsci calls it cultural hegemony. A hegemony is created by which the people think in a particular way, and it is created through many processes and structures of the society. Till this point, Gramsci stands with Marxism.

Gramsci says that the hegemony is so strong that for a revolution to be possible, we should challenge the hegemony. It means not just attempting to change the base and wait for the base to change the superstructure. The consciousness should be the issue to be addressed directly – to change the base.

Gramsci was modifying Marxism in the direction of Hegel's idealism – the idea that ideas change all the other things. The consciousness should be changed, to bring about a change in the base, to bring about a revolution.

Gramsci thought of something called counter-hegemony, which encourages the proletarian revolution. Essentially, Gramsci was asking the revolutionaries to think in terms of how to change the ideas and address the society with new ideas. He was advocating not to treat ideas simply as outcomes of economic processes.

This kind of thinking impacted many Marxists all over the world. Cultural hegemony refers to the domination or the rule maintained through ideological or cultural means. Because of this hegemony, many ideas which are convenient to the ruling classes or the bourgeois classes appear to be commonsense. For example, the idea that one can succeed if one tries hard enough becomes a commonsense idea though this need not be always true.

Gramsci thought one doesn't have to wait for the ripe conditions for a revolution to happen. This is what he said on the 1917 revolution, in December 1917: "In Russia, Marx's Capital was more a book of the bourgeoisie than the proletariat. It stood as a critical demonstration of how events should follow a predetermined course: how in Russia bourgeoisie had to develop, and a capitalist era had to open, with the setting-up of a Western-type civilization, before the proletariat could even think of its own revolution."

Marx's Das Kapital predicted certain things, but they did not happen, and Gramsci called the Russian revolution a "revolution against Das Kapital." It could happen because of Lenin, because of his not waiting for the conditions to mature.

Role of intellectuals

Gramsci discussed the role of intellectuals. For the revolution to be possible there should be a particular kind of intellectuals in the society. In Gramsci's time, some intellectuals thought that they were independent though many of them were embedded in the bourgeois ideology. They supported a particular kind of ideology that was conducive to the bourgeois classes. Gramsci called them organic intellectuals. This is similar to the present-day concept of embedded journalists. These organic intellectuals conveyed how capitalism is good or how the present is justified.

Gramsci thought that to create a counter-hegemony, we need to create organic intellectuals but they should be influenced by or embedded in the revolutionary ideology. These intellectuals should create a complete set of ideas, not just about the economy and the class struggle, but about the totality of the society. Gramsci was talking about how to use and how to change the social consciousness to create conditions conducive to revolution. One should alter the social consciousness and not simply the class consciousness. Gramsci was no longer thinking only in economic terms, he was thinking in terms of culture, culture as shaping the economy, the ideas, and the social institutions.

Gramsci and Mao

There is a lot of similarity between Gramsci and Mao. Mao's cultural revolution was a sweeping effort to change the consciousness of the Chinese people, to create a counter-hegemony. Mao thought that what he was doing was not enough, so he wanted to change the traditional consciousness. Mao's idea of the role of intellectuals also was similar to Gramsci's. The intellectuals were sent to the rural areas so that they would identify themselves with the peasants and think differently. Mao also connected the communist movement with Chinese culture and Chinese nationalism.

Gramsci was writing about similar things. "What a tragedy it would be if the groups of intellectuals who come to the working class and in whom the working class places its trust, do not feel themselves the same flesh and blood as the most humble, the most backward, and the least aware of our workers and peasants. All our work would be useless and we would obtain no result." Gramsci wrote this, and later Mao would implement it though he did not know about Gramsci.

Regarding nationalism, Gramsci wrote: "An elite consisting of some of the most active, energetic, enterprising and disciplined members of the society emigrates abroad and assimilates the culture and historical experiences of the most advanced countries of the West without, however, losing the most essential characteristics of its own nationality, that is to say without breaking its sentimental and historical links with its own people." This is nothing but 'sinification' of Marxism, which Mao implemented.

Gramsci's central idea is this: create a revolution through ideas and don't think only of economic change. In the decades that followed, when Maosim spread to many areas, Gramsci's ideas also spread along with it. For example, in Telangana, Gaddar's songs were intended to bring counter-hegemony. Gramsci's idea of creating a revolutionary consciousness was applied in the context of the Dalits too, and much literature has been generated for this purpose.

Change the consciousness, and do not wait for the economic changes. This notion is an important contribution of Gramsci. However, a limitation in Gramsci's thought is that counter-hegemony creates its own problems, as in Mao's state.

Gramsci did not think that hegemony as such was wrong, whatever be its purpose – pro-capitalism or anti-capitalism. Open communication is the solution to it. Gramsci was trying to substitute one kind of influence with another kind. As communist countries showed, counter-hegemony could be much worse than hegemony. Gramsci did not anticipate how hegemony could be bad in general, not just the hegemony that was supportive of the bourgeois classes.

Think on it

1. What do you know about the prison notebooks of Gramsci?
2. Why did Marx expect the communist revolution to happen at an advanced stage of capitalism?
3. Was Gramsci right in expecting a communist revolution in Italy?
4. What is hegemony in a social context? What is counter-hegemony?
5. How was the Russian revolution against Das Capital?
6. What is the role of intellectuals in creating a hegemony?
7. What role should intellectuals play in creating a revolutionary consciousness?
8. What are the similarities between Gramsci's thought and Maoism?
9. What is the problem with the counter-hegemony that Gramsci wanted?

Mao

Mao Zedong

CHAPTER TWENTY-NINE

Maoism: A Disaster of Epic Proportions

Maoism can be better understood not as a set of ideas, but as a set of actions done by Mao Zedong (1893–1976). Mao primarily went by Lenin's understanding of Marx but modified it to suit the Chinese conditions. Russia in 1917 was somewhat industrialized and had an industrial working class, the proletariat. Mao's China during the 1940s was much less industrialized than Lenin's Russia.

About 90% of the population of China at that time were peasants. Mao had to think of applying Marxism to an essentially agrarian country. Mao accepted Lenin's basic ideas: communism can be brought even in a backward country, one doesn't have to wait for capitalism to mature, and the party is needed for this purpose. Mao took all that, but the peasants would constitute the revolutionary force in Mao's China. Leninism applied to peasantry became Maoism.

Before World War II, the context of China was one of political instability just like that of Lenin's Russia. Two groups were fighting with each other: the nationalists who ran the government and the communists. There was an invasion by Japan. It was in these conditions that Mao had to work out his strategy, fighting both internal and external enemies.

The Long March of 1934, which was undertaken by the communists to avoid persecution by the Kuomintang government under Chiang, was a significant event in Mao's struggle. The communists were driven out of their rural strongholds and were forced to walk around 6000 miles to shift their base. Out of one lakh poorly armed peasants who set out on this march led by Mao, only 10,000 survived.

China's internal conflict was going around the same time as the external aggression by Japan. In what was called the Rape of Nanjing of 1937, 2-3 lakh Chinese were killed, and 20,000 women were raped by the Japanese army, according to a survey of Chinese history by the US government.

Between the communists and the nationalists, the communists were in a better position to fight the Japanese. The communists' resistance was peasant-based and their technique was guerilla warfare. Maoism revolved around peasantry, guerilla warfare, and was rooted in national identity. The way the peasants were mobilized to resist the Japanese contributed to the popularity of Mao. Unlike Lenin who used the existing situation to his advantage to set up communism, Mao played a major role in pulling China out of the chaos it had been in and in setting up a communist government. Mao is still revered among the Chinese for freeing their country from external enemies and creating a united China out of the chaos the country was in.

How did Mao mobilize the peasants? As was done by Lenin before him, by promising land reforms – which was understood as land being distributed to the peasants. But communism also involved collectivization. The land was first expropriated from the landlords. Millions of landowners were killed or imprisoned, and the land was redistributed to the peasants. Then between 1955 to 57, there was collectivization in China, just like the one that happened in the Soviet Union decades before. There were communes of up to 25,000 persons in each. Because of all this, a lot of dislocation took place, there were famines. Between 1960 and 62, millions of people starved to death. Only a little food was produced and even that was confiscated for the towns, just as it was done in the USSR earlier. Later the size of these communes was reduced, there arose smaller village-level units.

Mao's communism had the same flaws as the communism of both Lenin and Stalin. It was essentially undemocratic and unpopular. But Mao seemed to have believed that people approved of his communism. In 1956, when the Hungarian uprising shocked the world and showed the unpopularity of communism there, Mao thought that he should allow criticism of his communist rule. He said, "Let a hundred flowers bloom, and let a hundred schools of thought contend." Many messages were put on wall posters calling for sweeping changes. But Mao did not think that he should change, he only thought that the others should change. In a series of purges that followed, many critics were eliminated.

In what was called the Anti-Rightist Campaign, the critics were supposed to be reformed through labour camps and reeducation. Many of the surviving critics faced problems not only because of their criticism but also because of false accusations by others based on personal scores. Some party people were given quotas to identify the critics, who were now called class enemies.

Then there was what was called the Great Leap Forward of 1958-61. Between 1953 and 1958, a Soviet-style Five Year Plan had produced good results, but Mao wanted something more. He wanted faster results. He wanted rapid industrialization as well as collectivization. In the absence of an independent press, the officials reported higher steel yields and better crop yields during the 5 years, but in reality, the system was collapsing. Still, Mao did not think that his theories were wrong. He thought the culture of the Chinese society itself should change. He started the Cultural Revolution of 1965-69.

Mao provoked the youth to form what was called the Red Guards. These Red Guards memorized a little red book written by Mao titled Thoughts of Chairman Mao. The young people were supposed to implement the ideas of Mao and eliminate the critics and the cultural elements that were not supportive of Maoism.

During the Cultural Revolution, children reported against their parents, friends reported against their friends. People who were considered not sufficiently dedicated to Maoism were sent to labour camps and punished, many of them were killed. It was felt that the education, in general, was wrong, and the professors were humiliated, with some of them beaten publicly. The university campuses were closed. At hospitals, the doctors were asked to scrub the floors. Many people were killed as class enemies, for being insufficiently convinced of Maoism. This was totalitarianism – a personal dictatorship supported by an ideology. By the time of Mao's death, the state seemed to have failed in every way.

It was much later that a completely new regime under Deng helped China recover and make progress. Maoism was a disaster of epic proportions. It is a tragedy that it is still taken as a worthy ideology by some people outside China even at present. Why is Mao still popular in China? Partly due to propaganda and partly because he was the one who freed China from foreign occupation and created one nation.

Think on it

1. How was Mao's China different from Lenin's Russia?
2. Who were the nationalists in China?
3. How did China's communists win the internal as well as the external battles?
4. What was the context of the Long March?
5. What was the Hundred Flowers Campaign?
6. What were the consequences of collectivization in China?
7. How did Mao handle his critics?
8. What was the Great Leap Forward?
9. What was China's Cultural Revolution?
10. Was Maoism a big failure?
11. Why is Mao still popular in China unlike Lenin in Russia?

Hannah Arendt

Hannah Arendt

CHAPTER THIRTY

Banality of Evil

Hannah Arendt has some interesting and thought-provoking views on totalitarian regimes. She wrote on Nazism and Stalinism. She discussed the nature of evil in these regimes. She says the nature of contemporary evil produced through political systems is different from ordinary types of evil.

Hannah Arendt (1906-75) was born in Hanover, Germany, in a Jewish family. She studied at the University of Marburg, under Martin Heidegger. Around that time, Germany was experiencing a surge of antisemitism. In 1933, Hannah was briefly imprisoned for doing illegal research into antisemitism. She had to flee Germany. She lived in Paris for 6 years, working for various Jewish organizations. She faced problems there also. In 1940, she was detained by the French as an alien when Germany invaded France. She went to the US in 1941 and stayed there for the rest of her life.

She wrote The Origins of Totalitarianism in 1951. This got her instant recognition because the topic was new and she had command over the subject. In the same book, she also wrote on things like antisemitism and imperialism, but it was her views on totalitarianism that got her wider recognition. In 1958, she wrote The Human Condition, which is more refined than her first book and is considered her most accomplished work. These books established Hannah Arendt as an important Jewish philosopher in the US.

Eichmann trial

Eichmann was a top Nazi official and a major organizer of the Holocaust. After the war, he had fled to Argentina, but Israeli agents captured him in 1960 and brought him to Jerusalem to put him on trial. Hannah requested The New Yorker magazine that she would like to report on this trial. The New Yorker employed Hannah Arendt, a philosopher rather than a regular journalist. Hannah went to Jerusalem to report on the trial.

Hannah was interested in the job because she wanted to see a Nazi official, who was involved in many crimes, in person. She wanted to know how he would be like as she did not attend the Nuremberg trials. She was curious to see those people she heard, wrote and studied about.

What she found there was a total surprise to her. She thought so much about it without giving herself any time limit. Then she gave her account on the trial to the magazine, and later published it as a book in 1963, titled Eichmann in Jerusalem: A Report on the Banality of Evil. The subtitle ‘banality of evil’ became a famous phrase. What did she mean by it and what was her notion of evil?

Hannah went to Jerusalem expecting to see a monster in Eichmann. Hannah found a completely different person in Eichmann. She found him to be very dumb, rather silly. Strangely he did not have any strong views against Jews personally. He had thought that he was just doing his duty, following the orders coming from the top. He seemed to Hannah simply like a bureaucrat seeking promotion. If we look at the actions of such Nazi officials, they appear so monstrous. But the real person who was behind those monstrous activities did not look like a monster at all. Hannah Arendt wrote that Eichmann showed “no case of insane hatred of Jews, of fanatical anti-Semitism or indoctrination of any kind. He personally never had anything whatever against Jews.”

Eichmann did not complete his high school or do any vocational training and found his first significant job only through family connections. Hanna Arendt said that he suffered from a “lack of imagination" and an "inability to think". During the trial, he was sometimes bragging about things he did, though it would clearly hurt his defence. Hanna wrote that "bragging was the vice that became Eichmann's undoing". It showed how stupid he was. Six psychologists examined him and found no trace of any mental illness or personality disorder.

Some of Hannah Arendt's observations shocked people. She wrote: "Despite all the efforts of the prosecution, everybody could see that this man was not a 'monster', but it was difficult indeed not to suspect that he was a clown. And since this suspicion would have been fatal to the enterprise [his trial], and was also rather hard to sustain in view of the sufferings he and his like had caused to millions of people, his worst clowneries were hardly noticed and almost never reported."

She called the trial a show trial, managed by prime minister Ben-Gurion. She said Eichmann was being tried for crimes in retrospect because when they were being committed they were not crimes. He was being tried in a territory in which he did not commit them. She also criticized the Jewish councils for not doing enough to prevent the Holocaust. While they did not cooperate with the Nazis they also did not actively resist them. She was not very much criticizing Eichmann; instead, she was criticizing the Israeli government and the Jews. To many, it looked like blaming the victims.

What Hannah Arendt wrote has some theoretical implications. Despite being very controversial originally, her description of Eichmann withstood the scrutiny of time. This is a case where somebody goes to report an event, but the reporting becomes more significant than the event itself.

How could the evil that killed millions of people be called banal? Banal means very dull, ordinary, commonplace. She did not mean that the crime or the action in itself was insignificant, she only meant that the person who committed it was very ordinary. A very ordinary man was committing extraordinary crimes.

How are ordinary people able to commit such extraordinary crimes? That was the question that interested her. She felt this was a different kind of crime, because going by the crime, it was so huge; but when you try to find the criminal, there is no criminal.

She said that violence of such proportions is committed not by persons, but by people who lost their personhood. In 2013, they made a movie titled Hannah Arendt. In a scene in the film, Hannah was shown answering the criticism on her report, before a group of students. "A court had to define Eichmann as a man on trial for his deeds. It was not a system or an ideology that was on trial, only a man. But Eichmann was a man who renounced all qualities of personhood, thus showing that great evil is committed by "nobodies" without motives or intentions." To Hannah Arendt, conversion of humans into "nobodies" is in the very nature of totalitarianism.

Think on it

1. Why was Hannah Arendt drawn towards the study of totalitarianism?
2. What was the idea Hannah Arendt had of Eichmann before she met him?
3. What did Hannah Arendt find in Eichmann?
4. What is meant by 'banality of evil'?
5. How can evil be committed by 'nobodies'?
6. From the Eichmann trial, what can we know about Nazism?
7. Can the banality of evil be seen in the US presidents who were responsible for many deaths in various countries? Where else can we see it?

CHAPTER THIRTY-ONE

Totalitarianism: Is Personhood Lost?

Hannah Arendt's thinking on totalitarianism primarily revolves around an idea that can be traced to the etymological meaning of fascism. She used the idea behind fascism to explain totalitarianism. Her important contribution to the subject is that she combined both Nazism and Stalinism into one concept. That is an innovation because they indeed seemed to be two completely different systems. Hitler and Stalin were supposed to have hated each other, though they had a pact during WW2. Nazism is based on racism; Stalinism is based on communism. Hannah Arendt saw the similarity, how they are essentially the same though they seem to be two different ideologies.

Hannah Arendt viewed totalitarianism from the literal meaning of fascism. The Latin root of the word 'fascism', 'fasces', refers to a bundle of rods tied around an axe, it was an ancient Roman symbol of the authority of the civic magistrate. The idea is that each rod is weak but all of them combined become strong, like a single rod. There are different individuals, but they become a group, which behaves like a single entity.

This unity is the source of the strength. But the individuals lose their personality. Individuality ceases to exist because the various individuals have become one. All become one. It is a bundle of rods, there are no individual rods, they are fused into one. That is how they have transformed themselves from individuals to one collective entity. This phenomenon Hannah Arendt called totalitarianism. She felt that what was going on under Nazism as well as Stalinism was this kind of totalitarianism. The ruthlessness of the state was produced through the destruction of individuality.

Adolf Hitler (1889-1945) was born in Austria, he became the leader of the Nazi Party in 1921, and was the German leader from 1933 to 1945. His ideas were expressed in his 1925 book Mein Kampf (My Struggle). These ideas are essentially about antisemitism and the dream of German domination of the world. As a part of the agenda of world domination, the inferior race of the Jews had to be exterminated. This he set about doing from 1941.

Antisemitism refers to prejudice against or hatred of the Jews. Nazism was based on antisemitism, but Stalin's Russia had nothing to do with antisemitism. It was supposed to realize the ideals of communism. Joseph Stalin (1878-1953) ruled the Soviet Union from 1927 till his death in 1953. By 1938, there were 7 million Russians in the labour camps, according to an estimate by Robert Conquest. The survival rate in these camps was 2-3%. Going to a labour camp meant near-certain death. By 1953, the number of people in these camps rose to 12 million. About 1 million people were directly executed without being sent to the labour camps.

Loss of personhood

To Hannah Arendt, totalitarianism refers to "perpetual movement premised on the goal of total domination; it differs from despotism". It is a perpetual movement. It is supposed to be dynamic and has the goal of total domination. The distinction between private and public is not there. There is no civil society. Everything comes under the state. Terror is "the essence of totalitarianism, it abolishes any space for human exchange and all capacity for action." Loneliness is "the human condition under a totalitarian regime, where even private life is destroyed."

All of this is guided by an ideology. Ideology means "the logic of an idea, deducing complete reality from theoretical propositions."

If it was only a personal dictatorship, some would fear the dictator, some would be loyal to him, but there would be a limit to the dictator's control. If there is an ideology, the control becomes much more extensive, because more people will be indoctrinated into the ideology. One doesn't have to take the commands from the leaders, because one knows, going by the ideology, what one is expected to do in a particular situation. Ideology brings unity of action among millions of people.

It is not that Hitler murdered anyone personally. Nor did Stalin. Thousands of officials were employed in murdering people. What is the basis of the actions of these thousands? Not only that the orders were coming from the top, but also that these officials were indoctrinated by the ideology.

Hannah Arendt examines the basis of the Nazi ideology. She finds that this ideology does not have any reason. How could the Jews be the enemies of Germany or the world? How can we say that the Jews are a race? Jews are the people who did not accept Jesus as the saviour and so remained as Jews. Judaism is a religion. Why did they have to be eliminated?

Hitler looked at everything in terms of ideology. He made people think in terms of it. He used propaganda. Propaganda alone will not succeed. Independently thinking people should be terrorized into submission.

The ideologies of Hitler and Stalin were irrational, the reality of the world was being reduced to a set of simplistic ideas, and those ideas were forced on people through propaganda and terror. It was the ideology that is uniting the people, converting men into an unthinking unity.

Evaluation

Hannah explains totalitarianism in terms of the dissolution of personhood. I have a simpler explanation. Totalitarianism can be explained in terms of personal dictatorship plus othering. Othering means you create one group as the other, and make it an object of hatred.

The practice of othering excludes persons who do not fit the norm of the social group. To Hitler, the Jews constituted the other. To Stalin, certain classes constituted the other. It is about the other that hate generation is systematized.

At first, Hitler committed some murders simply to keep himself in power; then he made Jews the enemies, and created a system to eliminate them, and also developed a political goal for the Germans. The justification to realize the ideology became the justification for his dictatorship. Some people who were very close to Stalin had their family members sent to labour camps, but still, they were loyal to Stalin because they thought he was on a great mission, the mission of establishing communism.

Ideologies strengthen personal dictatorship and personal dictatorship enables imposing an ideology that doesn't have a rational basis on millions of people. Not only antisemitism doesn't have a rational basis, but the same was also true about communism too. What does communism have anything to do with sending millions of people to labour camps? Personal dictatorship plus eliminating the enemies would explain totalitarianism.

In democratic countries also, othering happens without any kind of personal dictatorship. For example, how do you explain the bombing of the Japanese cities by the US? So much violence was perpetrated by a democratic country. The US citizens too mostly approved of it. The American president at the end of the Second World War was not judged the way Hitler and Stalin were. The American president convinced many people that the Japanese deserved it. This is a case of othering plus democracy.

Othering brings the ability to kill. You don't have to be a particularly cruel person. Many are capable of inflicting violence based on othering when they think their actions are right. Many people are disturbed by what the Nazi officers did in the concentration camps. For example, in one incident, an officer noticed that a child of a Jewish mother was hidden in a suitcase. The officer suspected it and opened the suitcase, the child was there. He took the child out and to stop his cry, he hit him against the wall. The child died. Had the officer lost his personhood by that time? It is doubtful.

Persons can do horrible things even with their personhood intact when they think their actions are right. Man is like that. We are like that. Not just the people in totalitarian regimes.

However, a loss of personhood can be taken as a partial explanation in some cases. In ethnic rioting, for example, people may do things that they are incapable of doing individually. The same may be true in certain actions of security agencies where their uniform dress helps in losing personhood.

Think on it

1. What is the origin of the word 'fascism'?
2. What were the main ideas of Adolf Hitler?
3. What were the main aspects of Stalinism?
4. What is the role of ideology in totalitarianism?
5. Is personhood lost in totalitarianism?
6. Can men commit horrible crimes even in democratic countries?
7. Can loss of personhood be an explanation in certain cases of violence?

CHAPTER THIRTY-TWO

On Nations Devouring Human Rights

Hannah Arendt thought of human rights in terms of the relationship between men. Human rights don't exist individually for a human being, they exist between men. She takes the view that human rights are what are agreed upon, rather than some natural, intrinsic things. Because they are agreed upon, action should be taken to preserve them.

Since she considers totalitarianism as the idea of men fusing into one, plurality is a very important concept to her. "Plurality is the condition of any political life, defined by the fact that it is men, not man, who live on the earth." On human rights, she says: "The only given condition for the establishment of rights is the plurality of men; rights exist because we inhabit the earth together with other men. No divine command, derived from man's having been created in the image of God, and no natural law, derived from man's 'nature' are sufficient for the establishment of a new law on earth, for rights spring from human plurality, and divine command or natural law would be true even if there existed only a single human being." (The Burden of Our Time)

She discusses who should implement these human rights. She observes that these human rights are related to the nation. The nation gives citizenship, and human rights are protected through the rights of citizens. In India, for example, fundamental rights are given through citizenship, although some rights are given outside citizenship too.

Hannah Arendt says that soon after there was a declaration of human rights, the nations were also given sovereignty. This raises the question if a nation is not honouring the human rights of its citizens, what should the world do? If a nation persecutes its minorities, what should the world do? Hannah takes the position that the entity that gives rights to man is humanity itself and not a nation. It is the responsibility of humanity to take care of human rights.

Hannah Arendt personally suffered a loss of citizenship. She lived for years as a stateless person without any rights. She felt that people should not be subjected to such a situation. She considers certain crimes not as crimes against individuals but rather as crimes against humanity. "The right to have rights or the right of every individual to belong to humanity should be guaranteed by humanity itself" (Origins).

In Eichmann in Jerusalem, she wrote that the crimes committed against Jews were crimes committed against humanity itself. She felt they should have fallen under the jurisdiction of an international tribunal. "Russian concentration camps in which millions are deprived of even the doubtful benefits of the law in their own country, could and should become the subject of action that would not have to respect the rights and rules of sovereignty" (The Burden of Our Time).

Labor, work, and action

There are certain concepts such as labour, work, action and power that Hannah Arendt uses in a particular way. Humans are primarily engaged in three types of activity – labour, work and action.

Labour corresponds to the biological life of a human being, as a member of a species. Labour is done to maintain life, producing food is labour. The products of labour are consumed. Bread is consumed, whereas work is the activity that produces artificial things in the world. A computer is a result of work. This is also consumed, but it can stand for a longer time, independent of the one who produced it. Work is long-lasting. Work can be finished, labour is not. Labour is an unending activity, a continuous activity.

Hannah Arendt says that people in the contemporary world are more concerned about labour and work, and not action. What is an action for her? It is an aspect of expression, it is "the only activity that goes on directly between men without the intermediary of things and matter." It corresponds to the human condition of plurality. Romans used the words 'to live' and 'to be among men' interchangeably. People live with other people, and each person is different.

"We are all the same, that is, human, in such a way that nobody is ever the same as anyone else who ever lived, lives or will live." With each birth "something uniquely new comes to the world." But totalitarianism destroys plurality. Hannah Arendt thinks that each person is distinct, and communication between them, speech, or writing, to influence the other -- all that is action. It is not just about producing things. Writing a book is action. Calling for a revolution is action. Calling for social change is action. Influencing nation-making is action. Public-spiritedness is action. Man is expressing himself.

Hannah Arendt thinks that labour is at one level, work is at a different level, and action is at another level. As societies become more consumerist, they tend to be absorbed in labour and work, and not in action. That is her concern. The action can be contemplative, it can be political, or anything else.

Hannah Arendt also uses the word 'power ' differently. Power to her is not authority and not domination. She uses the word 'power' in the sense of empowerment of the people for concerted action. "Individuals, acting together with a common purpose, could create a new space of tangible freedom in the world, relying on nothing more than the power implicit in their own mutual promises and agreements." (On Revolution)

Power differs from domination when people join themselves together for the purpose of action. It is the ability to act in concert. It is a condition of politics. When human rights are violated or are likely to be violated, people should get together and act in defence of their rights.

Hannah Arendt, being a Jew, was a strong supporter of Zionism originally but withdrew her support to it later. She did not support the way Israel was being formed. She said that a Jewish state was being created at the expense of the Palestinians. She wrote about the need for Arab-Jewish cooperation, "without which the whole Jewish venture in Palestine is doomed." And also, such cooperation would show the world "that there are no differences between two people that cannot be bridged" (The Jew as Pariah).

In modern times, the concept of 'we' is becoming more important than being a member of an agreed-upon political community, which is a state. She calls this the conquest of the state by the nation. This kind of nationalism and reducing human rights to national rights had proved catastrophic. Citizenship should go beyond nationality.

Think on it

1. What is meant by human rights as a relational concept?
2. Are not human rights a result of natural law?
3. Are not human rights natural rights?
4. What is the relationship between citizenship and human rights?
5. Who should be responsible for the protection of human rights?
6. What is the conflict between national sovereignty and human rights?
7. What is meant by the conquest of a nation by a state?
8. Explain Hannah Arendt's concepts of labour, work and action.
9. How is power different from domination?

Rawls

John Rawls

CHAPTER THIRTY-THREE

Justice Is What You Want When You Do Not Know Who You Are

Man has been debating for centuries what constitutes justice. What do we call a just system? Capitalism is one idea of justice, communism is another. And what is justice in personal relationships? Normally it would seem like people have different notions on what constitutes justice. In this context, John Rawls came up with a particular conception of justice, claiming everybody would have the same notion of justice if a set of assumptions are made.

Why do people differ on what constitutes justice? Because they tend to think from the viewpoint of their interests. For example, what is a just man-woman relationship in a marriage? Men will have one notion and women will have a different notion. Rawls says that there is a simple way of getting to a consensus on what is a just relationship. When one doesn't know what one's gender is, what one would think about the just roles of man and woman would indeed be the just roles of man and woman.

A is selling something to B, there is a contract between A and B; a fair contract is the one in which A and B will agree when they do not know who may be selling and who may be buying. Not knowing your position will let you arrive at an idea of justice that would be agreeable to all. On this principle, Rawls proposes a theory of justice which he thinks is universally applicable.

John Rawls (1921–2002) put forward his views on justice in A Theory of Justice, published in 1971. In 1993, he wrote Political Liberalism. His heroes are Kant and Lincoln. He was from a wealthy family but from an area where slavery had been an issue, so he reflected on the moral issues of slavery at a personal level. His final work Justice as Fairness: A Restatement (2001) addressed the points raised by the critics of his 1971 work.

Original position

What is Rawls's theory of justice? There are two parts to it. The first part refers to what people should not know about themselves and the assumptions based on which they will base decisions on justice. This part is called the original position. The second part refers to the principles of justice they would agree to.

You don't know your class and social position, you don't know your gender, you don't know your abilities, you also do not know your likes and dislikes. Interestingly, you don't have any preconceived notions of what is good and what is bad. You don't belong to any religious school or philosophical school that tells you this is justice. This is what John Rawls called the veil of ignorance.

Under the veil of ignorance, you are to choose a society to live in, a society that distributes goods in a particular way. What you would then choose would be a just society. Rawls thinks everyone would make the same choices in this kind of situation.

This society is assumed to have moderate scarcity, there is a limited supply of goods, and these goods are not simply economic but also include rights, powers, opportunities, and the bases of self-respect. Since the society is of moderate scarcity, you don't get whatever you want and there is competition, people want more than what is available.

Also assumed is that a person tries to maximize the goods he has, he is risk-averse and is not gambling. He is non-envious too, he doesn't think in terms of how to reduce others' outcomes, he only thinks about how to increase his own outcomes.

It is not only about how the government is distributing, it is about how the society is distributing. Society may consist of religion, family, institutions of culture and so on. How are the social institutions functioning in a way that these goods are going to be distributed? What are the principles of distribution of these goods – regardless of who is distributing them?

Not knowing about yourself means not only not knowing your particular part – be it gender, caste, or social position – but also not knowing your abilities, likes and dislikes. You do not know whether you have those things that help you reach the top. You may or may not have them. Depending on your abilities, you may get the goods – goods being income, wealth, power, respect – in abundance or you may fail very badly, but you don't know about your abilities.

You don't know whether you have to work as a labourer or as a scientist or as a manager, whether you are going to be a man or a woman, and whether this society is going to have castes and classes, and if there are castes and classes, whether you are going to be born in a higher caste and higher class or a lower caste and lower class.

Also assumed under the original position is that once you make a choice, you cannot go back. You can't say, for example, 'See, I like mental labour, but these people are giving more importance to physical labour. I can't work in this system. I want to get out.' Once you enter, you cannot getaway.

Principles of justice

Justice is seen as the right way of distribution of goods. Rawls proposes these principles of distribution.

1. *Equal liberty. Each person is guaranteed a set of basic liberties.*

2a. *Equal opportunity. There must be equal access to jobs and services under fair equality of opportunity.*

2b: Difference principle: Inequalities are justified if they benefit the least advantaged members of society.

Liberty is the first principle, and then equal opportunity. Rawls says people will choose one more principle. In the original position, people would think, 'Suppose I don't have the required things to go to the top, or am not born in a higher position, the system should take some special care of me.' Rawls says that people want the difference principle only as of the last principle. To them, liberty comes first and equal opportunity next. In this above listing of Rawls's principles, 1. equal liberty 2a. equal opportunity and 2b. difference principle, the order of importance is *1 > 2a > 2b*

To create equal opportunities for everybody, one's liberties should not be taken away – as the communists did. Liberties are very important. Give equal opportunities. But there would be some who can't make use of the opportunities, offer special help to them. The difference principle should come only in the end.

These principles can be applied broadly across many areas. For example, you should have private schools because people should have the right to go to whichever school they want. Would not private schools generate inequalities? Is it not a violation of the principle of equal opportunities in the job market? Yes, it is, but private schools should be there because 1 > 2a. There can be special care in terms of reservations in jobs for certain sections, and this would be in keeping with the order of 1> 2a> 2b.

Inequalities

In an equal society, the top 10% gets and what the bottom 10% gets. This distribution is without reference to their abilities and their work. Rawls says people would not like it, because in case they have higher abilities and put in more work, they want to be at the top – to have more money, more power, and more respect. They wouldn't want to be a part of an equal society. Marxian communism is therefore not a just society.

People also wouldn't want a society where the top 10% gets a very high amount and the bottom 10% gets little. People don't want gross inequalities because in case they don't have the skills, they would get very, very little. So people do not want to maximize the maximum position – which is called the *maximax*.

Equality would be rejected and extreme inequality too would be rejected. People would prefer some kind of balance. In case they have an ability, they would like to move towards the top, but in case they don't have any they would like to be taken care of. They would prefer maximizing the minimum position – the *maximin*. The lowest 10% are better off in a just society than in any other society.

Just society

What kind of a political system will these principles lead to? The Soviet-type communism or a single party system is rejected because people do not give liberties. Unregulated capitalism is rejected because it does not take any special care of the weak.

One proposal is going for capitalism which generates growth as well as inequalities but using higher taxation of the rich for the welfare of the less privileged. But Rawls says, in that case, the rich people would think that they are working hard to benefit somebody else. That would generate a conflict between the rich and the beneficiaries of the welfare system.

Rawls argues for a different system. He calls for property-owning democracy. He got this idea from J. E. Meade. Rawls says more people should have productive assets and education so that we would first prevent inequalities being created, and then reduce the transmission of whatever inequalities created through the high inheritance tax. That, to Rawls, would be a just system.

Think on it

1. What would be a just marriage in terms of gender roles?
2. What would be a just contract?
3. What is the veil of ignorance?
4. What is the original position?
5. What are the three principles of justice?
6. What is the basis for the difference principle?
7. Is the communist society that Marx thought of a just society?
8. What is maximin? Why would people prefer that?
9. Should you have private schools that can violate equality of opportunity?
10. Why should you have reservations in jobs?
11. What is a just political and economic system according to Rawls?

Habermas

Jugen Habermas

CHAPTER THIRTY-FOUR

Does Capitalism Thrive on Traditional Values?

Jurgen Habermas (b. 1929) has written many books, some of his important works are The Structural Transformation of the Public Sphere (1962), The Legitimation Crisis (1973), The Theory of Communicative Action (1981) and The Crisis of European Union (2012). He wrote his first important book in 1962, and his most recent work was written fifty years after that. Recently some seminars were held on him, celebrating 'Habermas at 90 years'. He is a rare person who is in a position to make very insightful remarks on the contemporary world.

The thinkers of the past did not know about things like totalitarian regimes, the collapse of the USSR and the European Union. Habermas gives a theoretical perspective on some very important contemporary developments. Of the many things that he talked about, one concept became particularly important – the legitimation crisis.

A regime may lose its legitimacy, institutions may lose their legitimacy. The legitimation crisis refers to "a decline in the confidence of administrative functions. institutions or leadership". Habermas says, "The governing structures are unable to demonstrate that their practical functions fulfil the role for which they were instituted." Though the issue of legitimacy is an old one, the phrase 'legitimation crisis' was used for the first time by Habermas.

Crisis in capitalism

Capitalism is a particular kind of economic system that goes by the market principle. There are certain values by which capitalism works. One very important value is self-interest, other values include greed, profit motive, rationality, and individualism. When people are trying to maximize their self-interest, capitalism is supposed to work in such a way that the entire society is benefited.

We know that these ideas of self-interest, greed, profit motive are not values that were glorified by tradition. When Adam Smith talked about the positive use of self-interest, he was making a statement that went against tradition. Religions never glorified greed, self-interest, and the profit motive.

Rationality is another value of capitalism, it means calculating in terms of better outcomes and for the benefit of the individual. Individualism itself was a new value. Based on these new values, capitalism generated wealth.

This is what we normally think. But Habermas adds something very insightful to this. He says that what contributed to the success of capitalism are not only these new values but also many traditional values. He said capitalism was taking many things from tradition.

Capitalism might have focused on self-interest, but the people who started talking about self-interest were those who had been socialized into the idea of generosity and helping others. The people who were socialized into thinking in a particular way and who had certain values picked up the new value of self-interest. These people could not be completely preoccupied with self-interest. Self-interest may stand out saliently, but their moral basis was still the traditional value of generosity.

Capitalism calls for spending and consuming. The values of spending and consuming were new, but the people were socialized into restraint in consumption. For those who already had the value of restraint, consumption became an additional value.

Many traditional values are responsible for the smooth functioning of capitalism. For example, capitalism doesn't teach trust, but trust is needed for contracts to be fulfilled. Capitalism requires bureaucratic organizations where a person is loyal to his superior, but capitalism does not teach loyalty.

Individualism is a value that capitalism glorifies. But the value of individualism itself operates on the traditional value of giving importance to the community. The values that made capitalism work were not drawn from capitalism itself, they were drawn from the tradition. Max Weber said capitalism itself came from the Protestant Ethic.

Habermas says capitalism became so successful that it gave rise to a new kind of thinking and a new kind of man. In this process, it ate up its own source, which was tradition. For example, when everybody thinks in terms of self-interest, then the trust may not always be a good thing, loyalty may not always be a good thing. Deceiving at crucial times could maximize self-interest!

But if capitalism is based on purely rationalistic self-oriented calculations without any values, will it survive? When we say the society is changing, it means that the capitalist values are spreading over the society and the social values are changing. Capitalism is depleting its source, just as, one could say, the HYV plants depleted the nutrients of the soil and the water table.

If there are no traditional and pre-capitalist values to bank on, what would be the values of capitalism? Would demand and supply forces give rise to a just society? Does the market always reward merit? Does it always reward hard-working people? Does people's perception of justice match with the outcome of capitalism? There are enough reasons to think that it is not always so. The market delivers goods to those who can buy and not to those who need them more.

Social values and capitalist outcomes do not match with each other, and therefore one can expect the state to regulate capitalism. How should the state regulate? According to the values of society. But if the state intervenes beyond a point, it will affect the motivational component of capitalism. For example, if the state tries to enforce equality, then the incentive systems may be wrecked and capitalism can become less successful.

At present, capitalism is facing some very serious problems all over the world. Inequalities are one issue. In a very advanced capitalist society like the US, capitalism had legitimacy for over two hundred years because people believed that the market would reward the hard-working, the meritorious, and the inventors. But inequalities in the US are now at such a level that it is the accumulated wealth that is leading to more income and not merit and hard work. This means that the capitalist system is also not contributing to efficiency.

Creative destruction and rewarding the right people are considered merits of capitalism. That is no longer the case. People are questioning, what is capitalism doing? This is what is called the legitimation crisis. It is not only capitalism that can have a legitimation crisis, but socialism too.

How can we end the legitimation crisis in capitalism? What does Habermas think is the solution? Habermas thinks that undistorted and honest communication, where people are free to say what they think, will give rise to a new set of values. And only that way this crisis can be met.

Habermas says, "Bourgeois culture as a whole has never been able to reproduce itself from itself. It was always dependent upon motivationally effective supplementation by traditional world views."

What did capitalism depend on? "The repressive authority of conscience and an individual achievement orientation among the bourgeoisie and external super ego structures and conventional work morality among the lower classes."

The market is not doing what it is supposed to do. "Since it has been recognized even among the population at large that social force is exercised in the form of economic exchange, the market has lost its credibility as a fair (from the perspective of achievement) mechanism for the distribution of life opportunities."

The solution is a discussion of all the relevant issues. "How would the members of a social system, at a given stage in the development of productive forces, have collectively and bindingly interpreted their needs (and which norms would they have accepted as justified) if they could and would have decided on the organization of social intercourse through discursive will formation, with adequate knowledge of the limiting conditions and functional imperatives of society?"

The values the people would finally arrive at would be the right values. This is called the rational consensus theory of morality. And without new values, the alternative is force. "Our excursion into the contemporary discussion of ethics was intended to support the assertion that practical questions admit of truth. If this is so, justifiable norms can be distinguished from norms that merely stabilize relations of force. In so far as norms express generalizable interests, they are based on a rational consensus (or they would find such a consensus if practical discourse could take place). In so far as norms do not regulate generalizable interests, they are based upon force."

Think on it

1. What is meant by the legitimacy of institutions?
2. What is a legitimation crisis?
3. What were the new values that capitalism brought to society?
4. Mention the traditional values that capitalism used to create a better society?
5. What is the legitimation crisis in capitalism? What is its cause?
6. How should we respond to the legitimation crisis in capitalism?

Books Consulted

1. *Western Political Thought: From Socrates to the Age of Ideology* by Brian R. Nelson (2nd edition, 2004)
2. *History of Political Theory: An Introduction Volume I: Ancient and Medieval* by George Klosko (2nd edition, 2012)
3. *History of Political Theory: An Introduction Volume II: Modern* by George Klosko (2nd edition, 2013)
4. *Marx's Concept of Man* by Erich Fromm
5. *Political Thinkers: From Socrates to the Present* edited by David Boucher & Paul Kelly (3rd edition, 2017) (for Arendt)
6. *A History of Western Political Thought* by J S McClelland (1996) (for Hegel, Bernstein, Lenin)
7. *Introduction to Political Theory* by John Hoffman & Paul Graham [for Rawls]

9 798885 035330

Printed by Libri Plureos GmbH in Hamburg,
Germany